Sashiko Made Simple

Japanese Quilting By Machine

ALICE ALLEN

to Pam –
Enjoy every stitch
of Sashiko – It is
great fun –
Alice Allen '94

Bernina Books Limited

Illustrations by Sheryl Russel, Sherrod Designs
Photography by Kaz Ayukawa, K Graphics

Library of Congress Catalog Card Number: 92-70059
ISBN 0-9632175-0-X

Table of Contents

Foreword

Venturing forth into the world of book publishing has been an exciting, creative, inspiring, demanding, tiring, fun, and long process. It has been a year of excitement and frustration. But in the end...reward! Bernina Books Ltd. is born.

We, at Bernina of America, are very pleased with the first in our "How-To Series for Sewing Enthusiasts". Quilters around the world swear by their Bernina sewing machines. So what better technique to introduce first than an ancient form of quilting - Sashiko, Japanese quilting. The pure simplicity of sashiko design is beautifully and easily translated from a hand technique to the sewing machine. And the unique features of the Bernina sewing machine make this stitching technique a matter of just sitting down to sew!

Alice Allen has captured the beauty of sashiko through her designs and finished projects. From the smallest coin purse, simplest book cover, to the most elaborate coat, she has transformed the basic fabric through her stitching. Alice's talent lies not only in the written word but also in her sense of style, her feel for line and design, and in her handling of the sewing machine. Follow her through this book and discover for yourself the beauty and charm of sashiko.

JoAnn Pugh
Marketing Manager- Software
Bernina of America

Acknowledgements

Writing a book is never a lonely project. The writer engages and depends on multiple people and talents to reach the end of her task.

Many students and friends have encouraged me along the way. Among those I specifically thank:

JoAnn Pugh, who was there at the beginning and gave endless hours and adept handling - an editor extraordinaire.

Bernina of America, Inc. for their belief in this project.

My Bernina Support Group: Kathy Embry for her enthusiasm, each Sewing Specialist for their friendship and sewing expertise, Nancy Bednar for her quick, professional stitches, Dianne Kemper for her great presentation ideas, and Kaz Ayukawa for his beautiful photography.

Sheryl Russell, my tireless friend and artist, who made every stitch look perfect.

Teri DeBolt, for her beautiful sample sewing.

My family, Charles and Alisa, for the dinners eaten out, the clothes folded and the unending love.

My mom, for the pages edited and the soup cooked and dad for his perfect templates.

My friends in the stitching world, who believe in me as a friend, teacher and designer and continue to ask "Alice, will you…?" I always say "yes."

Introduction

Sashiko entered my life about three years ago when JoAnn Pugh, Marketing Manager - Software for Bernina of America, Inc., asked me if I knew about *sashiko* and suggested I research the techniques for classes. I was actively teaching machine embellishment methods in quilt conferences and had become aware of beautiful book resources about hand-sewn *sashiko*, but...they were all printed in Japanese. With research, I did find a few sources printed in English (see References).

As with many needle art forms, *sashiko* developed from a need to conserve and repair scarce fabrics. The history interested me, but the techniques and designs intrigued me most. I found myself mentally transposing hand stitches to machine stitches. I asked myself, "How attractive would the designs be sewn in strong machine threads on denim?" I knew I had to meet the challenge.

The hand threads are comparable to machine cordonnet. Ancient indigo is duplicated in modern denim. With experimentation I knew *sashiko* (pronounced *sah-shih-koh*) could take many forms. White cordonnet thread on denim mimicked the traditional; metallic thread on silk revealed the potential of *sashiko*.

I began teaching machine *sashiko* at workshops and received enthusiastic response from my classes. I soon discovered I needed more material and decided to develop a workbook format suited to the new machine *sashiko*.

This book is the result of that effort. You can follow the chapters and progress from learning to use heavier thread in your machine, to advanced interrelated patterns on your favorite jacket or wall hanging. Projects can range from a simple motif on a square to many *sashiko* designs on one fabric. Matching thread colors can carry a motif, or blended colors can be stitched.

Consider *sashiko* as a new, adaptable, creative machine form. It is quick and easy; it is beautiful. Both the novice and experienced seamstress can successfully sew *sashiko*. Bernina is a perfect tool for this craft, as the stitch quality, tension and needle adaptability is unlimited. Select a great fabric, your favorite pattern (the hardest part) and follow my step-by-step machine techniques for *sashiko*.

CHAPTER 1

Sashiko - Doing Stitches

S *ashiko*, literally "doing stitches", is a Japanese stitch form, a blending of embroidery and quilting. Originally, dexterous stitchers labored for many hours to mend, strengthen and conserve fabrics using the running stitch. Their techniques developed out of the necessity to extend the life of their garments, constructed of loosely woven bast (grasses or tree bark) fiber fabric of that era.

These loosely woven fibers, worn by the commoners of the Tokugawa shogunate period (1603-1865) were ignored by members of the upper class. Instead silk, wool and cotton textiles maintained their status and usefulness among the wealthy. This hierarchy of fiber availability maintained a separate style for the cultural classes. Toward the close of this historical period cotton was introduced to the common people of northern Japan and immediately appreciated, although it could not be cultivated in the cold, northern climate.

Instead, the fabrics were preserved with sashiko, a simple running stitch, sewn through multiple layers of the precious cotton fabrics. Sashiko not only preserved the fabric in a beautiful manner, but provided strength, warmth and a resistance to abrasion. Sashiko stitching became readily apparent on the worker's garment, but eventually was seen on additional household items, and even the tabi, or two-toed sock.

The straight stitch is the simplest and quickest of all stitches. The hand needle runs in and out of the fabric in evenly spaced thread rows to form a solid filling and to create texture within the design. Referred to as running stitch, the stitch is sewn with a coarse cotton thread in a long hand needle (2 1/2") with a sashiko thimble in a simple push-pull rhythm of needle to fabric. The needle eye rests against the thimble, allowing numerous even stitches (stitches of same length and space) to be worked in a continuous row in the most efficient route, with every stitch worked evenly. Sashiko stitch beauty and quality are determined by the evenness and straightness of stitches.

The basic running stitch, worked in predictable rows, eventually gave way to elaborate patterns interpreted from kimonos and environmental influences. The simple straight stitch became beautiful rows of thread, twisting and turning into brick and herring-bone patterns, bamboo and grass shapes. Foliage and animal motifs found a comfortable presence among the furrowed rows of straight stitches.

Sashiko stitching is often referred to as both quilting and embroidery. Sashiko embroidery is traditionally sewn on a single thickness of indigo dyed fabric. When worked through multiple layers, the textured stitching is identified as quilting. In recent years, traditional indigo dyed yardage sewn with white thread has enjoyed renewed popularity as a modern technique in Japan and internationally. Sashiko stitches have appeared on everything from utility bags and totes to modern clothing and home accessories.

Transferring hand running stitches to sashiko by machine is simple. The choices in threads, needles, and stitch variations retain the best of sashiko, revealing its beauty in the classic quality of even machine stitches. Technology adapts perfectly to tradition. The essential criteria of quality sashiko stitching - evenness and durability - is easily executed in machine stitching. Stitches connect to one another and form traditional sashiko patterns. Machine stitched sashiko is sewn in continuous rows, often referred to as "grid patterns" or "continuous line sewing". Beginning at the edge of a marked line, grids and motifs are quickly sewn in an orderly fashion. Each machine stitch width and length can be changed as needed or variety achieved by joining decorative stitches with straight stitches. Computerized functions easily utilize several stitches at once. Joining decorative stitches with straight stitches and combined automatic machine functions increases the dimension of machine possibilities.

One of the strengths of Bernina sewing is flexibility. Options are readily available with every stitch. Exclusive features such as the automatic presser foot lifter simplify pivoting and moving the fabric. Adaptability to assorted thread weights and needle sizes permits variations of traditional sashiko. The traditional white thread on blue indigo is not mandatory. Today's market is alive with thread colors and textures suited to every project. The many options open new and exciting avenues. For example, red pearl cotton thread grid stitched across purple silk noil fabric is also a choice for sashiko work, and a grand twist on the traditional.

Today, the focus of sashiko is far different than the running stitch of the shogunate period. With machine stitching, the sashiko patterns adapt to clothing and crafts, and best of all, are easily executed. With time, functional sashiko became a classic art form. Now machine stitched sashiko opens new horizons.

CHAPTER 2

Sashiko...Equipment and Materials

Sashiko stitching translates readily to even-weave fabrics, basic sewing supplies and simple machine stitches. It is classic beauty in heavy thread sewn on denim. And it is equally tasteful sewn on elegant fabrics with versatile machine stitches.

The stitches are the same, with either choice requiring elementary supplies - rulers, marking tools and patterns. Variation in sashiko appearance develops as the stitcher selects heavy white thread on denim, or the more advanced possibilities of multiple patterns and interrelated threads.

Listed below is a reference to the sashiko supplies. Refer to Chapters 3 and 5 for detailed information on fabric choices and preparation, and machine set-up. See Useful Addresses for trade mark products.

GENERAL SUPPLIES

Top Thread -Traditional
    Cordonnet, topstitch,
        buttonhole twist
    All purpose polyester
    Cotton-covered polyester
    Cotton/silk finish
Top Thread - Decorative
    Rayon
    Metallic
Bobbin Thread - Decorative
    Cordonnet
    Decor™
    Burmilama™
    Rayon pearl
Measuring Tools
    Ruler - transparent plastic
    Triangle
    Protractor

Compass
Graph paper
Marking Tools
    Chalk wedge
    Fabric pencils
    Air/water soluble pens
    Pouncer
    Hera (scoring tool)
    Tracing wheel and paper
    1/4" masking tape
Stencils - Templates
    Designed paper/plastic
    Circle shapes-template
    Square shapes-template
Sewing Machine
    Straight/zigzag model

Presser feet:
    General purpose
    Multi-motion
    Open Embroidery
    Freehand Embroidery
    Cordonnet
    Circular Embroidery
        attachment
Topstitch needles -
    size #90/#100
Optional:
    Extra bobbins
    Black latch bobbin case
        for decorative threads
General Sewing Tools
    Scissors (5" and 8")
    Thin, long straight pins
    Size 18 tapestry needle

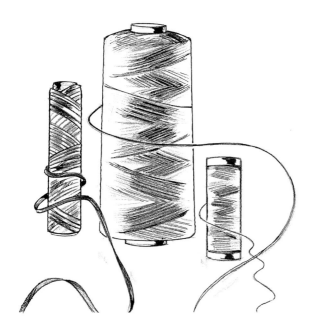

DESCRIPTIVE INFORMATION ABOUT SUPPLIES

THREADS

Begin accumulating supplies by selecting threads in color and texture to match fabric. Traditional sashiko design is strong in a high contrast thread to fabric; gentle in matching or blended color.

Many machine sewing threads are adaptable to sashiko stitching. Bernina choices of needle size, tension or bobbin adjustment provide alternatives to match the end project. For example, traditional sashiko is sewn with a thicker thread (cordonnet) on the top in a topstitch needle, supported by general purpose polyester or cotton-covered polyester on the bobbin. Sashiko sewn with rayon on the top is a non-traditional approach requiring polyester on the bobbin. Sashiko sewn with ribbon thread on the bobbin requires polyester on top. The final thread appearance is a choice variable to your taste, and each decision is customized with simple machine adjustments.

Top Threads. . .Traditional

This grouping of threads - cordonnet, topstitch, buttonhole twist - is thicker and gives prominence to the stitch. Typically a cord-like thread, these specific threads are available in cotton or cotton-covered polyester. These threads are strong, but beautiful with a soft luster.

Another topstitch option is sewing with two threads through the eye of one needle. Handled as one, two strands of 100% cotton/silk finish or cotton-polyester thread in a large-eyed (topstitch size #100) needle permits flexibility in color selection and thread impact, and gives the appearance of a thicker thread.

Top Threads . . . Decorative

In the last few years rayon and metallic have become thread choices for utility and decorative sewing. These threads are available in an array of color options, accessible to custom match sashiko fabrics, or provide unique color statements. Both rayon (30/40 wgt.) and metallic (40 wgt.) create sheen and shimmer and are designed to be sewn with the machine needle, or on the bobbin.

Bobbin Threads . . . Decorative

Some projects demand a heavy thread. Thicker high-twist threads or yarn-like threads, too thick for the needle, are better suited to bobbin threading. With the sashiko patterns drawn on the wrong side of the fabric, the motifs are easily stitched with novelty bobbin thread. The fabric is placed under the machine needle, right side down, and voila! the textured thread stitching enhances the design. Numerous threads are available for bobbin technique, as discussed before. Follow the bobbin procedure in Chapter 5, Machine Set-up, for specific sewing procedures.

Major thread companies (see Useful Addresses) provide brilliant metallics, thin and flat configurations and woolly textures. Some examples are Decor™, Burmilama™ and Pearl Crown Rayon™. Vibrant thread colors in a variety of shades add distinctive dimension to each project when used exclusively, or as an accent. It works well to interrelate novelty threads to traditional threads; stitch one sashiko area with a classic thread, then emphasize another with a textured or high-sheen thread.

To Mark The Design

Sashiko patterns are marked on the fabric with one of two techniques. If the design is a motif (floral, animal, crest, etc.), traditionally it is traced from a stencil made of paper or plastic. If it is gridded with angular lines, a ruler, plastic circle or square templates, or other geometric tool and chalk is used to transfer the design. Both pattern methods are marked directly on the fabric.

Stencils-Templates

Sashiko stencils (patterns) are available in pre- marked plastic from local quilt shops or mail-order catalogs. Many design options are available, ranging from traditional Japanese to American patchwork to very modern. Assorted sizes are obtainable and patterns can be adjusted to a specific size by enlarging or reducing on a copy machine.

Stencils can be traced or custom designed

by drawing individual patterns on freezer or typing paper. To create the paper stencil, place the paper drawing under the presser foot of an unthreaded machine. "Sew" along the design lines with a straight stitch allowing the needle to pierce the motif. The perforated design lines are used to transfer the design to fabric (see marking tools). Note: Do not use onion skin or tissue paper for needle piercing technique; they are not heavy enough.

Measuring Tools

Rulers, curves, triangles and pre-cut geometric templates are used to mark the straight and curved lines of sashiko. With each design line chalk-drawn adjacent to another, and directly on fabric, transparent plastic styles are the best choice.

Ideally, rulers of 12"-15" length in 1/4" grid marked on both ruler edges permit easy, repetitive marking. A 4"-5" ruler marked in a 1" grid is also useful.

Marking diagonal and curved lines is easier with equilateral triangles and 180 degree protractors. If possible, select several sizes. Pre- cut templates (circles, squares, etc.) are ideal tools. A marking pencil is preferred for softer circle motifs, such as waves and grass. Plan geometric shapes on 1/4" or 1" graph paper for increased accuracy.

Marking Tools

Sashiko grid designs are marked on fabric with an appropriate transferring pencil or chalk and ruler. Always check removable quality of marker to individual fabric. Some marking alternatives are:

1. *Chalk wedges* - a triangle shaped chalk. Draws a thin line in white, blue, pink and yellow. Brushes away on most fabrics.

2. *Fabric pencils* - easily sharpens to a fine point. Use like a drawing pencil. Available in white or silver.

3. *Felt-tip pens* (air and water soluble) - adaptable to marking detail, but may remain permanent on some fabrics.

4. *Pouncer* - made of fabric or felt. Used with a pierced stencil to imprint design on fabric.

5. *Hera* - scoring tool used to indent a line in firm fabrics. Pressure is applied with the plastic tool (shaped similar to point turner) while guiding along sashiko pattern. It is also used with tracing paper.

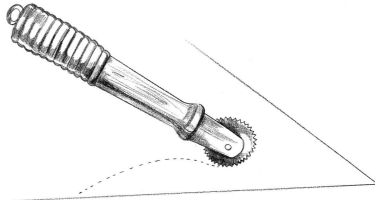

6. *Tracing wheel and paper* - used to transfer markings from pattern to fabric. A colored chalk-like paper is placed between cloth and pattern. The paper color imprints the fabric when wheel is pressed against it. Check washability of color marking.

7. *1/4" masking tape* - designed for quilters, the tape is useful for temporary marking.

Always select marking tools to match the sashiko design. One marking technique is not appropriate to all designs. Remember, grid or ruler designs are usually marked with chalk and ruler, ornamental motifs with stencil and pouncing technique.

GENERAL SEWING TOOLS

Use items from your sewing box for general sewing procedures and finishing. Certain sewing supplies are particularly helpful with machine stitching sashiko techniques.

Machine stitched sashiko requires many threads to be pulled to the fabric underside and tied. A large-eyed (size 18) tapestry needle facilitates thread returns, and saves fingers. Many threads in a large project can make sore fingers!

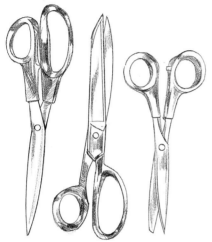

Scissors

To trim the tied back threads, use small (about 5") sharp-to-point embroidery scissors. The 8" scissor is necessary when cutting project pieces.

Joining units together is best accomplished with flat, long straight pins, as the pins sharpness and flatness is convenient when handling fabric at the sewing machine. Sewing machine set-up and the use of topstitch needles (size #90/#100) is covered in Chapter 5.

SEWING MACHINE

Traditional sashiko patterns are sewn with a straight stitch. All sashiko patterns are possible with a quality straight stitch, although zigzag and computerized memory stitches enhance the traditional appearance. Decorative stitches sewn singularly and in groups are also attractive.

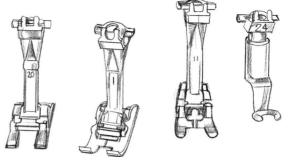

Presser Feet

The general and multi-motion presser feet are suitable for traditional sashiko sewing. Sewing feet designed with an open center are ideal for many rows of stitching as they enhance the visibility of stitch rows as they intertwine. The Open Embroidery foot is designed for grid sewing, while the Freehand Embroidery foot is recommended for dropped feed-dog stitch techniques.

Circular Embroidery Attachment

Accessories such as the Circular Embroidery attachment add a spark to traditional sashiko stitching. Vary the circle size from 1" to 14" in increments of approximately 1/4". The circle motif can be sewn in a straight, satin or decorative stitch. Interrelated or framing circles are easily sewn to enhance sashiko patterns.

Another presser foot, the Cordonnet, is grooved on the under side to accurately secure heavy threads used in sashiko sewing. It is ideal for rows of grid stitching.

To equip the machine for decorative threads sewn on the bobbin, purchase several extra bobbins. The thicker threads wind less yardage on individual bobbins, so it is convenient to have multiple bobbins filled in the same thread.

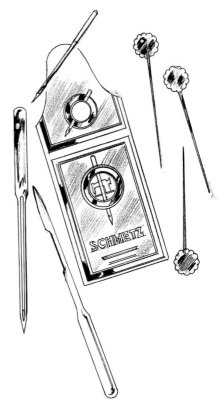

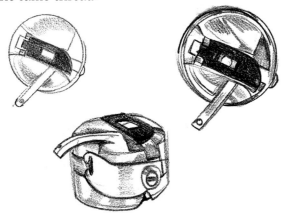

The Black latch bobbin case is designed with a black latch for easy identification. Often the tension screw is slightly adjusted for decorative threads. With the Black latch identification, it eliminates the confusion of tension adjustment between normal weight and decorative threads.

Topstitch needles with longer eyes are ideal for the thicker sashiko thread. Select the needle size (#90 or #100) to coordinate to thread and fabric.

All of the supplies are easily and inexpensively assembled. Many of the items are basic to the sewing room; used in sashiko machine sewing they acquire a new life.

CHAPTER 3

Fabric…The Background For Machine Stitched Sashiko

Complementary selection of supplies is necessary with each sashiko project. Each fabric and thread, sashiko pattern and style must interrelate and become one design. If these supplies are carefully chosen, a sashiko piece will be a joy to construct, and beautiful for years to come. Use this chapter as a guide to select fabric and related textiles, the background of machine stitched sashiko.

Fabric selection is a fundamental decision. Its individual character and end use plays a vital relationship to the project. For example, a sashiko embellished tablecloth can be sewn in a simple medium weight cotton. A sashiko trimmed jacket can be sewn in the same medium weight cotton, but usually needs additional interfacing and, if warmth is required, a batted inner layer. Each project started with the same fabric, each required different supplies for the end use.

Today's market offers many fabric options that reflect individual taste in quality and style. To assure positive beginnings, consider textile choices, then refer to the following questions and confirm personal decisions.

1. Is the fabric quality worthy of sashiko stitched embellishment?
2. Is the fabric a color to enjoy for a long time?
3. Is the weight and weave of the fabric complementary to the sashiko stitch technique?
4. Is the proposed project flattering to the fabric, and classic in styling?

If each question is answered yes at the beginning of the project, disappointment with distorted stitches and fabrics, tiresome colors and textures is avoided.

FABRIC SELECTION

Medium weight fabrics, in plain and twill weave are proven and appropriate choices for machine stitched sashiko. Natural fiber fabrics (cotton, wool, silk, linen) with dull, flat textured yarns enhance the coarseness and simplicity of sashiko stitches. Synthetic fibers (rayon, polyester, nylon, etc..) are most successful for sashiko projects if blended with natural fibers (rayon/linen blend). Synthetic advantages of care and wrinkle resistance are complemented by the dull, flat textured characteristics of natural yarns. Avoid 100% synthetic fabrics as they tend to be shiny, prone to pilling and generally less attractive for sashiko stitching.

Many fabric choices are available in plain and twill weave structures. Ideally suited to sashiko stitching, these weaves serve as the background, a stage for sashiko stitching. Identify the specific differences.

Plain Weave

Suited to long wear and decorative embellishment, a plain weave has an even thread count; the same number of threads are woven in the lengthwise (warp) and crosswise (weft) direction. Sashiko stitching complements the simple fabric structure. Plain weave yardage is woven in natural

and synthetic fibers with common names of sheeting, broadcloth, homespun (cotton), linen (flax), and noil (silk). It is woven as narrow as Japanese kimono fabric (14 inch) or as wide as wool flannel (52 inch).

Twill Weave

An equally complementary background is the twill weave, particularly when woven as a

cotton denim. The most durable of all weaves, diagonal ridges form across the fabric (often subtly) as the weft interrelates to the warp. Denim or jean fabric is similar in coloring to ancient indigo. Made of coarse, twisted ply yarn, it is distinguished by colored warp and white weft yarns, and varies in width from 45 inch to 60 inch. The indigo appearance of denim is a perfect stage for the sashiko stitch.

PREPARATION AND CARE

After fabric selection, the first step to machine stitched sashiko is fabric preparation. Evaluate the project's end care to decide the necessity of prewashing. If the finished project will be laundered, prewashing is a cautious decision. If the finished project will be dry cleaned, the fabric may only need pressing prior to stitching the sashiko patterns. Regardless of laundry or dry cleaning decisions, prestraightening fabric is usually necessary. Consider each project separately and preshrink or straighten as necessary.

To Preshrink Yardage

The word preshrink means treating the fabric (prewash) prior to cutting to inhibit shrinkage. Always treat the fabric according to its end use. If the finished project will be laundered in warm water, then prewash in warm water. If dry cleaning is the end care, preshrinking may not be necessary. Decide with each project, not if the fabric is washable, but if the construction is washable. Example: Denim is washable, but the beautiful sashiko stitching may have longer life with dry cleaned, not washed care. Therefore, since dry cleaning is the end care, preshrinking may not be necessary.

To Straighten Yardage

The decision to preshrink comes early, as does the decision to straighten the weave of cloth. To straighten fabric simply means to redirect the warp and weft threads to perfect right angles. Often, through the manufacturing process, loom weaving results in the horizontal (weft) thread setting "crooked" to the vertical (warp) threads. If the yardage is "off-grain" the fabric stretches or sews bubbly. To straighten grain, the fabric is pulled, from side to side, diagonally across the bias. Pulling the woven threads diagonally from selvage to selvage rearranges the warp and weft threads, setting the threads at right angle, straight one to another. To insure straight of grain:

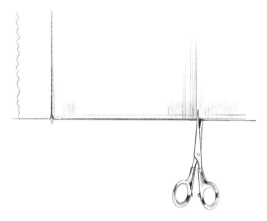

1. At the cut ends of fabric, clip into the selvage, then pull the crosswise thread from the clip to opposite side. If the fabric is loosely woven, pull the thread the total distance. If the thread breaks, prick edge for a new beginning, then repeat across the total width of fabric. If the fabric has torn edges omit this step; instead, refer to the torn edge as an accurate crosswise gauge.

2. Next, fold the fabric in half matching selvages. If the fabric folds evenly (near rectangle), the fabric is considered straight. Carry on with the sashiko project. If it folds with edges uneven to each other, then the fabric should be straightened. Pull the fabric on the bias, pulling diagonally from short end to short end, realigning the "off grain". When fabric is as "near rectangle" as possible, the process is finished.

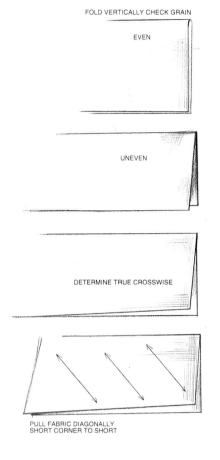

FOLD VERTICALLY CHECK GRAIN

EVEN

UNEVEN

DETERMINE TRUE CROSSWISE

PULL FABRIC DIAGONALLY
SHORT CORNER TO SHORT

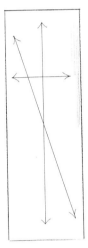

FABRIC GRAIN CORRECTED

Advantages of straight of grain:
- Straight of grain cloth is cut and sewn with less stitch pulling and distortion.
- Vertical seams hang straight and perpendicular down sides and back of garment.
- Each stitch sewn falls across a true perpendicular weave, reducing puckers and stretch.
- Straight of grain insures straight projects!

INTERFACING, UNDERLINING AND BATTING SELECTION

Typically, tablecloths, napkins and scarves use a single thickness of fabric. The design is worked on the single thickness but may require a stabilizer while stitching. Many other items such as bags and totes, hats and pillows, jackets and vests, require an inner layer of support of interfacing, underlining and/or batting, and are finished as a multiple layer (e.g., denim with batting).

In Chapter 8 specific supplies, including the inner layers of support are listed with each project. Identify these common and sometimes confusing terms - interfacing, underlining and batting as optional inner fabrics, used to make the sashiko project more functional and attractive.

Think of interfacing as a secondary (under) fabric or material used to provide support to the outer fabric. Fusible interfacing applied to the back of yardage gives body to the fabric, and prevents the fabric from stretching while sewing the sashiko rows.

Underlining gives softer support to sashiko stitching without adding density. Prewashed and straightened muslin and flannelette are good choices. Cut the underlining to fit the outer sashiko fabric, then pin baste thicknesses together. Stitch sashiko patterns through the double thickness, as if it were one. The fabric body will enhance the stitches.

Batting, as related to sashiko use, is a layered, dense material made of cotton, synthetic or blend. Available in different loft densities, it is placed under the fabric to provide padding and/or warmth.

Select interfacing, underlining and batting using these guidelines:

INTERFACINGS

Many interfacings are available to the stitcher. Designed to support primary (outer) fabric, fusibles are ideally suited to machine-stitched sashiko. Fusible interfacing is sold in widths from 27 inches to 60 inches; the most available is 27 inches. Common colors are white, beige and black. One of the best choices for sashiko is fusible knit tricot. It supports the fabric, yet maintains a soft hand.

Preshrinking fusible interfacing decreases the possibility of a bubbly outer appearance.

For extra assurance, and after preshrinking, it is also wise to fuse the interfacing to a fabric sample, to check the compatibility of fabric to interfacing.

To preshrink fusible interfacing, immerse the fusible interfacing into a basin of warm water for 20 minutes. Squeeze excess water out of yardage and hang on towel rack to dry. It is handy to preshrink several yards at once, storing unused portion for future use.

To fuse: With a steam iron apply preshrunk interfacing, fusible side down, to wrong side of preshrunk, straightened yardage. Place a damp cloth over the interfacing and

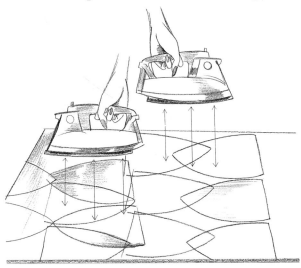

fabric, then apply heat in a strong up and down motion. Avoid moving the iron back and forth, as it stretches the yardage.

UNDERLININGS

Underlining is a secondary fabric placed behind the decorative outer fabric. Sewn together with the outer fabric, the second layer gives support and body to the garment. Select underlinings to match fabric choice and garment style.

Options include:

Muslin - firm, plain weave cotton suitable for lightweight support, without warmth. It is available in cotton and cotton/

polyester blend. Select either one, prewash and straighten.

100% cotton flannelette - ideal for lightweight, low-bulk warmth. It is a soft, warm fabric with a napped finish. Select only 100% cotton in this weave. It is critical to prewash and straighten.

BATTINGS

Another secondary fabric option is the addition of batting. Batting is not needed for all sashiko projects, but can add dimension, warmth and beauty to outerwear, home accessories and selected craft items. It is typically chosen for jackets, vests, totes and hats. Select batting designed to resist weeping or pilling (showing through to outer side) under sashiko stitched fabric. Read the packaging label for advice on prewashing or needle readiness for each project. If batting is a chosen support material, mark the sashiko designs on fabric as a single thickness, prior to batting. The softness is difficult to mark on.

To select appropriate batting, decide on the end use of the project. For moderate warmth, batt the front and back of garment, but not the sleeves (sleeves may only need an underlining). For outer wear, or hats and totes select batting for the total garment.
Consider:

Low-loft polyester - designed specifically for washability and low density appearance. Easy to use, resists pilling and gives warmth.

Low-loft cotton/polyester - ideally suited to clothing. Gives soft, quilted appearance. May need prewashing.

Other helpful support products include stabilizers that easily wash or pull away after stitching. Some options include:

Water-soluble stabilizer - a thin sheet suitable for sashiko support. It is ideally used for motif stitching. Draw the design on the water-soluble stabilizer, mount to sashiko outer fabric. Stitch motif with chosen threads, then immerse the fabric. The stabilizer will "wash-away", leaving only the thread design.

Pull-away stabilizer - available in light and medium weight, it is best used for sashiko stitching on craft or home dec projects. The paper stabilizer gives support to stitches, but may be difficult to "pull-away" from multiple rows of stitching. It is also available as a "press-away" product. It is lightly pressed to back of fabric, then pulled away after stitching is completed.

Freezer paper - available in most food markets, freezer paper stabilizer is suitable for light support of sashiko stitching. Place to wrong side of fabric, stitch sashiko, then pull or trim paper away.

Progression of sashiko stitches on a great fabric, one line to another, builds excitement. Many choices of fabric styles and textures are available. Never be afraid to experiment with fabric, color and design. A good choice justifies the quantity of time spent, and the quality of beautiful stitches.

Transferring Design to Fabric

Sashiko design choices become reality when drafted to fabric. Typically, designs are transferred to fabric with chalk or pencil, but tracing wheels, loose powder or cinnamon - even fabric scoring (creasing) can be used.

Motifs (floral, animal, crests, etc.) and geometric (walkways, mosaics, etc.) designs are transferred to fabric in different ways. The shaped motifs are usually transferred to fabric with a stencil and powder, while geometric designs are drawn on the fabric with ruler and chalk.

SELECTION OF MARKING TOOLS

The most important marking criteria is removability. Since fabric care and marking tools interrelate, the choice of marking color and method is individual to every project. Some markings can be washed away, others wear away with gentle brushing, and still others do not disappear. Carefully and individually, chose the best transfer method for every project.

Removability of markings can be accomplished in several ways. Light hand brushing or gentle washing will remove most markings. A powder that brushes away usually disappears with moderate handling while sewing, thus little post care is necessary.

Another option is washing. If that is a choice, consider using Orvis Paste, or a similar mild concentrated fabric cleanser. Specialized cleaners are found in most quilt and fabric shops. Dry cleaning is a third choice, but may not remove markings. It is best used for general cleaning.

SELECTION OF MEASURING TOOLS

With reference to Chapter 2, assemble assorted measuring tools, stencils and templates. Rulers that show on dark and light fabric, with 1/4" markings that read on both sides of rule are needed for all grid patterns. Curved and diagonal markings use protractors and triangles in different sizes, and a simple (school-style) compass that interchanges pencil colors. A very helpful tool is the circle template with precut circle shapes ranging from 1/4"-2 1/2". Available in craft/art supply stores, select the drafter's template with imprinted markings at each quarter. Circular repeats are easily drawn with this tool. Templates in other available shapes (squares, triangles) may also be helpful. Stencils for motifs are available from sashiko supply catalogs, but also consider traditional quilting stencils, or original designs.

Each measuring tool is necessary. Selection is made as each design is categorized into motif and geometric styles.

MOTIF DESIGN

Motif marking is best accomplished with a needle-punched stencil and pouncing pad. It is a neat and accurate method; makes transferring a complex design a simple chore. Tracing paper with a wheel is another option.

Stencils - To use stencils more than once, and save wear on stencils in books, trace the designs onto a piece of paper. Prepare the stencil by needle-punching holes on the design lines with an unthreaded sewing machine. Set machine for straight stitch, length of 3, and with Open Embroidery foot (#20), "sew" around stencil design. The unthreaded needle pierces holes in paper. If the design is shapely, sew around the shapes with the Freehand Embroidery foot (#24), feed-dogs down. Move the paper stencil design evenly, aligning the needle to stencil markings.

Pouncer - To construct pouncer, cut an eight inch square of 100% cotton fabric. Place approximately two tablespoons of cinnamon (to mark light fabrics) or talc (to mark dark fabrics) in the square center. Pull corners of fabric together like a hobo sack and tie.

Next, carefully alight paper stencil to desired position on fabric and pounce powder into dot openings. The powder transfers to fabric, in a neat and orderly fashion, in a series of dots. Connect the powdered dots with a removable fabric pencil.

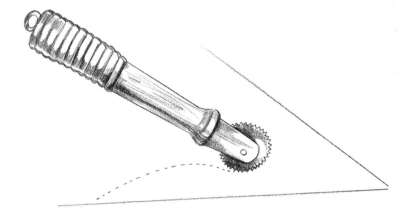

Tracing Paper and Wheel - An alternate motif marking tool is tracing paper with a wheel. Place removable tracing paper face down, between paper design and fabric. With tracing wheel, trace around motif, transferring design to fabric with the transfer paper.

GEOMETRIC DESIGNS

Geometric designs are transferred to the fabric in two ways. A common and simple method of transfer is with ruler and chalk. A light chalk grid can be drawn directly on fabric. Another method, suitable for "difficult to mark" fabrics, is the graph paper transfer. Designs are sewn from paper or stabilizer drawings directly to fabric.

Direct Fabric Marking - Drawing a grid directly on fabric is a convenient and quick way to mark sashiko designs, since it eliminates graph paper. One advantage of direct marking is the design cannot "shift" or slip out of position while sewing. With quality chalk wedges, "erasure" of lines is usually possible. To keep the chalk wedge sharp, shave edges with a potato peeler.

To begin:

1) Select sashiko design from traditional patterns (Chapter 6).
2) With chalk wedge, draw a "background" one inch square grid vertically and horizontally across graph paper. Select grid scale desired (1-2 inch) and draw lightly. If covering a large area of cloth, consider drawing one section at a time. The chalk wedge lines have a tendency to disappear and will fade in handling and sewing.
   Hint: To keep the square grid accurate, align the ruler with pre-printed markings on cutting surface for each new line. This prevents the grid from "growing."
3) With contrast chalk wedge color, draw the sashiko design variation across the background grid. It is not necessary to "redraw" the actual grid lines, draw only the diagonals, curves, etc. that create the pattern. Refer to pattern while sewing to accurately stitch the straight grid patterns.

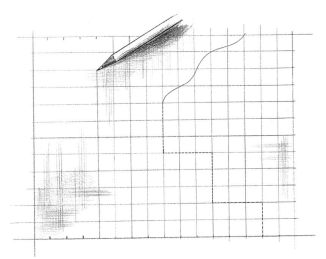

Graph Paper Transfer - A graph paper transfer can be drawn on any scale, but a one inch to two inch grid (spacing) is attractive on most projects.

To begin:

1) Draw a "background" one inch square grid vertically and horizontally across graph paper. These lines become the basis for the actual sashiko design.
2) Then, following a design from traditional patterns (Chapter 6) draw the design across the paper grid lines in contrast pencil. Mark the design as it "reads" - e.g., 2 up, 2 over - to match the design chosen. The completed design can be transferred to fabric, or used as a reference while stitching.

Alternate Transfer Methods - equal, repetitive grids can also be stitched with alternate marking methods. Consider:

Hera Marking - This straight plastic scoring tool is suitable when fabric has a tight weave. Place cloth on top of cutting board, then with gentle pressure, pull hera toward fabric edge. It will leave an imprinted indentation, ready for stitching.

Sewing Machine Seam Guide - Fitted to the back of the general sewing foot, it is ideal for sewing repetitive geometric designs. The seam guide is adjustable up to two inches and measures accurately from the last stitch line.

PLANNING DESIGN SPACE

Sashiko designs can be as simple as one motif in a corner of fabric, or multiple, forming a series of "all-over" designs, as on a jacket.

If marking more than one motif on fabric surface, plan sashiko design spacing on paper. Experiment with assorted ideas.

Symmetrical design (exact repetition of design in equal spaces) is classic and beautiful, but also consider asymmetrical spacing. The design will be different but complementary as it sets across the fabric. Plan sashiko space divisions on each project fabric with strips of narrow (1/4") masking tape placed in assorted arrangements across fabric.

Try these ideas:

- Consider arranging sashiko diagonally, one to another, and mark the grids in different directions for interesting results.

- Create an element of surprise in the sashiko design. Sew a sashiko design 1/3 in front, then finish on back, the lower edge or the opposite sleeve.
- Stitch sashiko in a checkerboard design, repeating the motif every other square. The element of fun is the different approach to a traditional design!
- Stitch curved motifs next to squares.
- Plan thread color and texture contrast for emphasis.
- Mix fabric colors, weaves and patterns.
- Stitch a sashiko design on a patterned fabric.
- Mix traditional sashiko designs with traditional quilt patterns.

Remember, classic and expected sashiko design is always beautiful, but the unexpected approach has exciting potential. Plan, experiment and enjoy!

CHAPTER 5

Machine Set-up

A quality automatic machine straight stitch is the primary character of machine stitched sashiko. Selected fabrics and threads appropriate to the design are the embellishment twist.

From these basics, it is fun, and even desirable to use zigzag and decorative stitches and, if available, computerized features of double stitch length, mirror image, and patterns in sequence. Choices of different needle and thread plus machine options add another dimension and an opportunity to explore the machine in a new way. Begin machine set-up with needle and thread.

TOP THREAD TECHNIQUE

Choose needle and top thread (see Chapter 2) together. They must be compatible, of first quality and designed for the project. The traditional look of sashiko - thicker thread - demands a larger-eyed needle for proper thread feed. If a thicker thread is sewn with a standard # 80/12 needle, the thread has a tendency to shred and break while sewing.

NEEDLE SIZES

Topstitching (Schmetz-N system) needles are designed with an oversized eye, appropriate for the thicker threads. Available in sizes #80/12, #90/14, #100/16, and #110/18, select the needle equal to fabric and thread thickness. Remember, the higher the needle number, the smaller the thread number (e.g., use #90 or #100 topstitch needle with 30 weight cordonnet thread). Refer to your machine guide (e.g., BERNINA'S MY GUIDE, VOLUME 1) for specific needle system information.

Charted below is specific needle information for Bernina machines:

Thread	Needle	Style
Cordonnet	#90/14 #100/16	Schmetz N Topstitch
#8 pearl cotton	#100/16	Schmetz N Topstitch
Rayon - 30 wgt.	#80/12	Schmetz H General purpose
Metallic	#90	Schmetz H General purpose
Silk finish cotton -50 wgt.	#90	Schmetz H Topstitch
(Two strands through one needle eye)		

Select the proper needle to match the machine, thread and fabric - always start with a new needle. Insert the needle into the machine properly (flat side usually to rear) and up as high as possible.

If stitching problems occur they are often needle related. Check for a dull needle, incorrect needle size/type or damaged needles. The wrong size or type needle (too long or short) can cause havoc in stitching.

TENSION

Tension is balanced when the stitch formation locks the top and bobbin thread evenly, between two fabrics, and creates an even thread appearance on front and back. Balanced stitches are a harmonious combination of a clean machine, a quality needle and compatible top and bobbin threads.

Decorative top threads (e.g., pearl cotton) used to sew sashiko require polyester or cotton-covered polyester on the bobbin. The bobbin thread must be strong enough to hold the stitch formation of the thicker top thread.

Tension adjustments - Sew a sample with threads chosen for sashiko project, then adjust the top tension if necessary. On some fabrics, the stitch formation may be pulled evenly, while on others the top thread may loop to the underside, or the bobbin thread may be looped to the top side.

Bernina's needle tension dial, located on the front of the machine, is easy to change. The higher the number, the tighter the top thread. The lower the number, the looser the top thread.

If the top fabric side shows a visible bobbin thread, decrease the top tension by moving to a lower tension dial number. The top thread is too tight.

If the under fabric side shows a visible top thread, increase the top tension by moving to a higher tension dial number. The top thread is too loose.

Adjust the tension dial in small increments of 1/2 number or less. When sewing decorative top threads, adjust the top tension only.

DECORATIVE BOBBIN THREAD TECHNIQUES

Another sewing option is to reverse the traditional sashiko stitching technique by placing decorative thread on the bobbin and general sewing thread on the top. The sashiko designs are sewn from the reverse with the decorative thread showing on the underside of the fabric. Simply draw the sashiko design on the wrong side of the fabric, or, if desired, on a pull away stabilizer. With the design now marked, place fabric under the machine needle "face down" (wrong side up). Stitch the sashiko design exactly on the drawn pattern. The accuracy of this technique is a distinct advantage of decorative bobbin thread stitching.

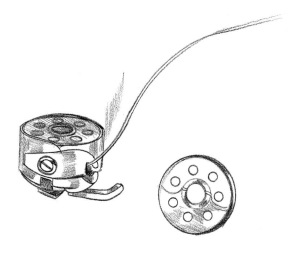

BOBBIN CASE

To begin decorative bobbin thread sewing, purchase an alternate bobbin case, suited to tension adjustment. Keep the "regular" bobbin case from the machine balanced for general sewing thread. A second bobbin case is preferred, so the tension can be altered to match decorative threads as needed. Bernina makes a Black latch bobbin case for easy identification. Use it for decorative thread adjustment.

THREAD

Select decorative thread - cordonnet, #8 pearl cotton, metallics, ribbon floss or any variety of novelty threads and fill the bobbin. Because the threads are thicker, the bobbin holds less thread. If the project is large, wind several bobbins to avoid the inconvenience of rewinding in the middle of the project. Wind the thread onto the bobbin slowly and evenly. Fill the bobbin approximately 3/4 full.

TENSION

Insert thread-wound bobbin in the bobbin case, placing thread under the tension spring. Pull the thread slowly, in clockwise position. It should pull like a normal thread, or slightly looser. If it grabs, or pulls tightly, loosen bobbin screw slightly. Turn left to loosen; turn right to tighten - remember, "lefty loosey, righty tighty". Adjust the bobbin tension screw in small increments of 1/4 turn or less. Be careful not to loosen the adjustment screw too much or drop the screw. (Refer to MY GUIDE bobbin case and bobbin instructions.)

PRESSER FEET

Sew sashiko with the presser foot suited to the project. Several appropriate Bernina feet include:

1. *Straight Stitch and Zigzag foot #0* - A general purpose foot designed for straight and zigzag stitches up to 5.5 mm.

2. *Reverse Pattern #1* - A multi-motion foot designed for all machine stitches that move forward and backward. The wide opening is ideal for beautiful satin stitches.

3. *Cordonnet #11* -
Designed with a grooved underside, it holds the cordonnet thread in exact alignment while sewing. The foot is also ideal to construct narrow corded finishing.

4. *Open Embroidery #20* -
Shaped like a U, it gives complete visibility and control. It is grooved underside to manage decorative thread. Easily used for grid stitching.

5. *Freehand Embroidery #24* -
Designed in an open circular shape and slightly shorter, to set just above the fabric, so the fabric can be moved freely. The foot has a hopper-spring mechanism to prevent fabric flagging. Used with the feed-dogs down, it is ideally suited to motif stitching. Also available is a companion-styled darning foot in a closed circular shape, foot #9.

6. *Circular Embroidery attachment* - A perfect accessory to create various circular sashiko designs. Adjustable to different dimensions of circles up to 14 inches, it is usable for circular grid motifs and as outer "framing" of sashiko designs.

Many of the sewing feet have multiple use, and are ideally suited to general sewing, machine applique and embroidery projects.

OPTIONAL MACHINE FEATURES

An advantage of sashiko stitching on the Bernina is the multiple sewing machine features that make stitching easy and enjoyable. Always use every feature available on the machine. The convenience of the carefully designed components save time and energy. They are simple to use and, in some models, can be recorded in memory for repetitive use.

Useful sewing machine features include:
1) Good lighting - Adequate visibility on both sides of the needle prevents shadowing.
2) Needle stop down - Machine stops in/out of fabric as stitcher releases foot control. Stitches do not coast another stitch.
3) Presser foot lifter - Raises and lowers presser foot with the knee for continuous "hands-on" sewing.
4) Needle positions - Five fixed needle positions that can be used on all stitches.
5) Long stitch - Stitches made every other stitch, is ideal with heavier sashiko threads. Can combine with other stitches for decorative combinations.
6) Computer features - With the advancements of sewing machine technology in the past few years, memory options are readily available on newer models. Options include:
a) memory and storage of stitch patterns - patterns can be altered and remembered in

a series for continuous use.

b) mirror imagery - asymmetrical stitch designs can be reversed in a continuous or alternate series.

c) variable speed - DC motor gives stitch by stitch control. Full speed and 1/2 speed options. Lower speed does not decrease motor power.

d) double length patterns - doubles the number of stitches in any pattern without losing stitch density.

e) single pattern - utilize one stitch at a time or a series of stitches in a single group.

f) pattern begin - starts all stitches at beginning cycle when pattern has been interrupted.

Modern sewing machine features are easy to use and definitely "consumer friendly." Match sewing machine options to individual sewing needs. Don't let a poorly equipped sewing machine stifle design creativity or limit flow of ideas.

Grid Patterns

Stitch grid with white thread.

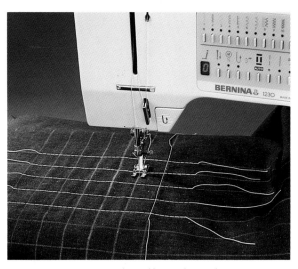

Begin new row with yellow thread.

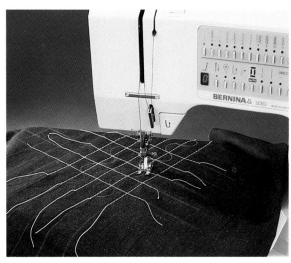

Add interest using the Net pattern with red thread on square grid.

Motif Designs

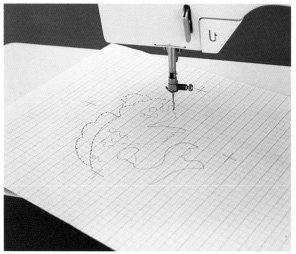

Create paper stencil by sewing, minus thread, around design.

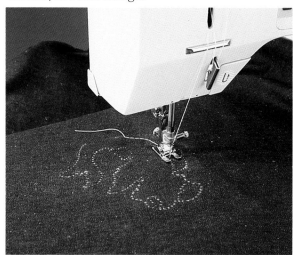

Stitch around pounced design creating motif.

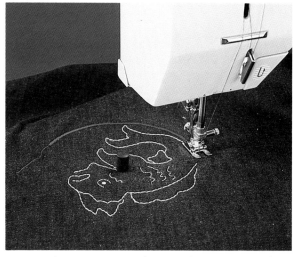

Frame design in a circle motif using Circular Embroidery attachment.

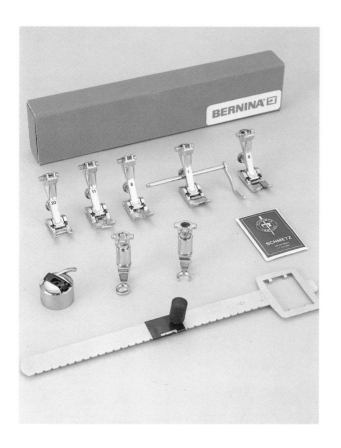

Machine accessories, fabric and thread.

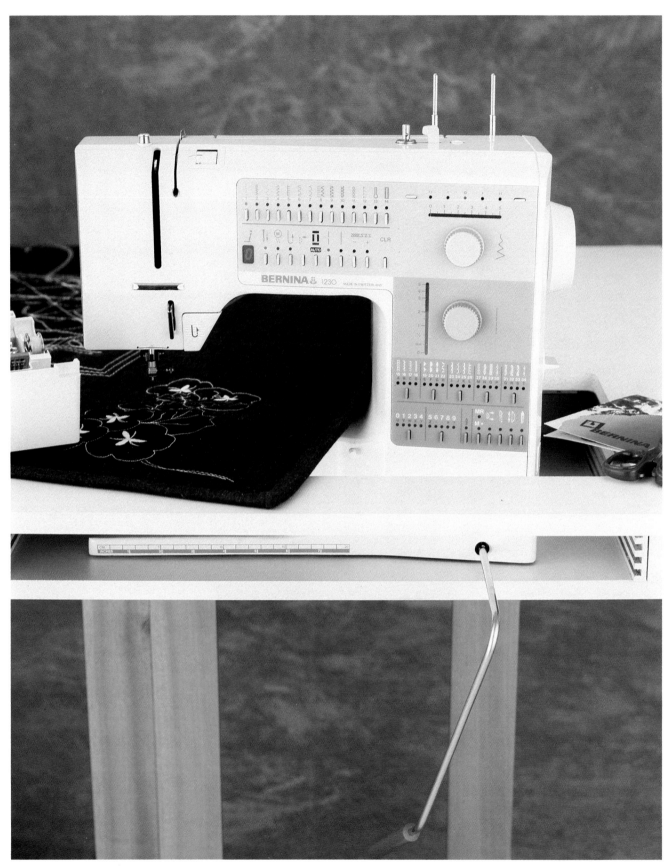

Bernina 1230 and accessories.

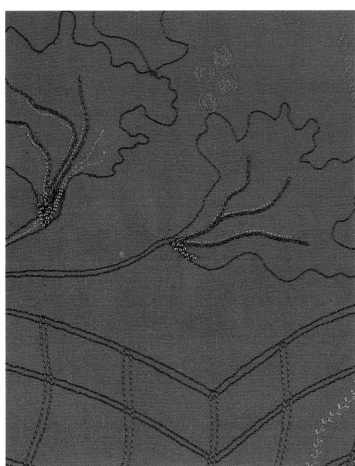

Red vest with floral motif.

Sashiko pocket on tote and cosmetic bag.

Drawstring Tote

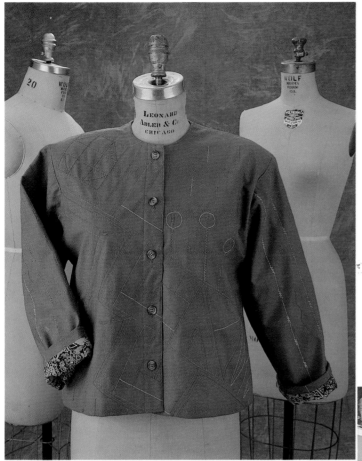

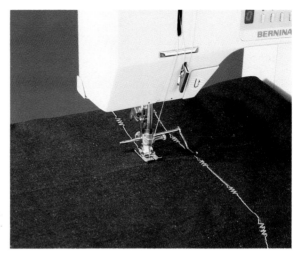

Create parallel rows of stitching using the seam guide and machine memory.

Green silk jacket with traditional patchwork interpretation.

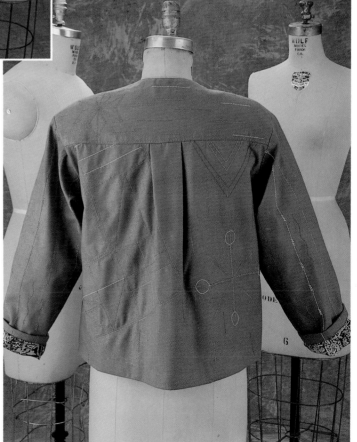

Memory capacity designs custom sashiko fabric.

Sashiko patterned fabric on large tote.

All-weather coat (front view)

All-weather coat (back view) with fan motif.

Coat detail:

Motif with preprogrammed memory
stitches and eyelets.

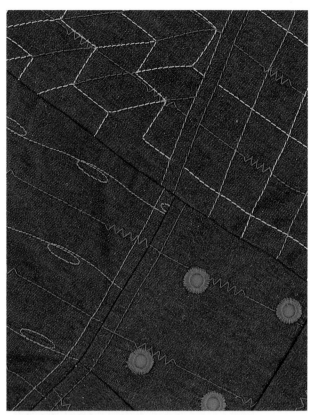

Arrow Feathers and Open Square patterns.

Variation on the Hexagon pattern.

Diamond within Diamond and Counterweights
pattern.

Pillow squares inset with sashiko.

Pillow squares inset with circled sashiko.

Patchwork sashiko designed place mat.

Tablecloth topper with sashiko grid and motif border.

Wall Quilt

Custom Book Covers

CHAPTER 6

Grid Patterns in Sashiko

Sashiko grid stitching is simple. It is repetitive rows of thread stitched horizontally and vertically in classic beauty and order. It is also repetitive rows sewn in variable modifications of curves, slants, spirals and zigs and zags.

Each design can be utilized alone or in multiple arrangement one to another. One thread strand of color is attractive worked row after row, while an interrelated palette of color creates differences in light reflections and sashiko moods. The very temperament of the sashiko piece is detailed in the stitch closeness, the action of the stitch and the fabric chosen for the project.

Each stitch line, alone or in multiple arrangement, forms a design of symbolic communication. Vertical lines suggest strength and formality, while horizontal lines are more informal, accessible. Diagonal lines hint of tension, a transitional tie between the upright and perpendicular lines. Curves produce energy, always a contrast, either relaxed or restless, controlled by the slant of the curve. Sashiko stitched spiral lines suggest movement unending, while the zigzag suggests excitement and energy. Every stitch line, depicted straight or curvy, wavy or broken movement, communicates a timeless, classic organization of pattern, in traditional sashiko fashion.

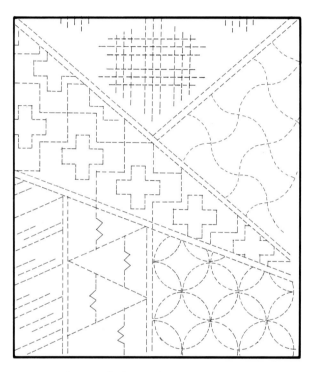

HOW TO STITCH A CLASSIC SASHIKO GRID PATTERN

Sashiko stitching is easily sewn with a quality machine. To sew traditional sashiko grid patterns, or for a unique design follow these simple steps:

EQUIP SEWING MACHINE…

1. Clean sewing machine. Oil, if necessary.
2. Insert new needle to match fabric and thread (traditional sashiko requires a topstitch needle, size #100, for cordonnet thread sewn on medium-weight fabric).
3. Place appropriate sewing foot on machine (Open Embroidery, Cordonnet, etc.).

4. Thread needle. Contrast thread color is traditionally sewn on fabric (e.g., white is traditionally sewn on indigo-blue fabric). Thread bobbin with polyester thread, matching the fabric color for bobbin thread visibility in each stitch. This *thread break* is complementary to the traditional hand look of sashiko.

5. Set stitch width - 0
   Set stitch length - 4

6. Refer to Chapter 5, as necessary.

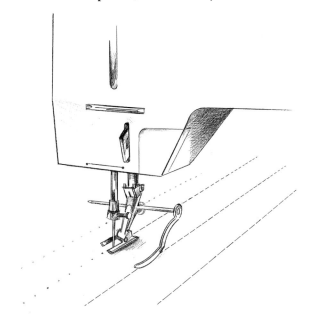

SELECT FABRIC…

Make fabric choices to match each project. Refer to Chapter 3 for guidelines.

TO STITCH SASHIKO…

1. Insert needle in grid-marked fabric. Pull bobbin thread to top side of fabric, then place top and bobbin thread under presser foot to the back. Begin stitching the chosen sashiko grid design.

2. Refer to the pattern chart to stitch each row. Stitch grid pattern in a continuous row as far as possible without cutting threads. When necessary to stop and cut threads, leave a thread tail of four inches to pull to back and tie. Stop, cut and pull thread tail to back and tie. If the pattern arrangement permits, sew along the outer edge to the beginning of the next row.

3. Begin the new row, stitch grid pattern. Stitch the next row, then the next, etc., until the design develops.

SOLUTIONS BEFORE PROBLEMS

Sewing techniques are always easier if questions are answered before they arise. Refer to the following guidelines to master stitch precision and explore the scope of sashiko design possibilities:

Beginning a Stitch Row - If the beginning is at the edge of a seam or on an outside edge, the beginning thread tails will be anchored in the seam allowance. If the stitch beginning is in the middle of the cloth and the thread tails will not be *hidden*, then leave a thread tail about four inches long at the beginning of each row. Stitch the row, then pull the top thread to underside. Tie it and the bobbin thread together, snug to the fabric. Trim excess tail to 1/2 inch.

Continuous Stitching - A term applied to stitching a design row(s) as far as possible without cutting threads. Always stitch each sashiko row in a continuous line, as far as possible, to decrease number of thread tails necessary to pull back and tie.

Corners - A primary strength of sashiko stitch appearance is each clean, precise corner. Utilize the needle-down machine function to control the needle. Stitch to a corner, stop, needle-down, then pivot and begin stitching the next direction. Needle-down permits "square turns." Utilize the presser foot lifter to raise the presser foot at each corner and use hands to turn fabric.

Hint: Often the stitch length chosen is just "ahead or behind" the actual drawn grid line. Make a decision to be uniform and consistent at every pivot, by stitching the same distance to grid every time. If the needle must intersect the exact chalk line, use the machine advantage of the presser foot lifter to rearrange the fabric to exact position.

To Join One Row to Another - Many patterns require "filler stitches" or short rows of stitches between long continuous rows. Insert needle *precisely* at the desired location, leaving a beginning tail of thread. Stitch to end of row, cut and leave four inch tail of thread. Move to next short stitch unit, repeat, until all short units are finished. Pull all top threads to back and square knot, snugly to fabric. Trim to 1/2 inch.

Changing Thread Colors - Sew one color in all the desired rows, stopping and cutting each thread, then move to next stitch location. When that color is finished, thread machine with new thread color and sew it continuously in each desired location. Match the bobbin thread to fabric to eliminate multiple bobbins. Always begin and end with a four inch tail of thread. Pull each top thread to fabric back, square knot and trim.

Pulling Threads to Back and Tying - To secure thread tails, pull cordonnet thread to underside by pulling bobbin thread, or, if desired, insert thread tail into #18 darning needle. Insert threaded needle into fabric at end of last stitch row. Push thread to underside, with needle intersecting the exactness of the last stitch. Tie cordonnet and bobbin thread in square knot, snug to fabric. Trim tails to 1/2 inch.

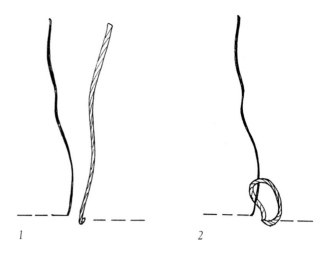

1 2

3

Correcting an Error - Stitch error is always a possibility. The stitches may be in the wrong place, wrong color, etc. If necessary to remove, clip the row in the middle of the length needed to be removed. Remove the bobbin threads in each direction from clips to desired location. Pull the top threads to back and tie snugly to bobbin thread.

MACHINE ADVANTAGES

- uniform stitch length
- presser foot lifter assists in pivoting at corners of each stitch turn
- presser foot designed with easy visibility of each stitch row - multiple feet available for individual projects
- memory capacity permits creativity - repetitive cycles of stitch patterns

SASHIKO GRID DESIGNS

Sashiko grid designs are categorized in like units. Most designs are based on a background grid of a one inch line marked continuously in vertical and horizontal rows across the fabric. Squares, diagonals, diamonds, hexagons and circles form the majority of the categories, with many variations and combinations.

Continuous interrelated rows of many of the designs make the traditional sashiko patterns adaptable to sewing machine techniques. Generally patterns are stitched in steps. For example, the length of a predominate line is stitched first. The short "filler" rows are added, with threads secured on back after a series of rows are stitched.

Basic marking tools of chalk, ruler and template, plus machine precision of stitch length accuracy form a base for grid motifs. Add unlimited machine pattern choices, and the seam guide on the presser foot for continuous straight lines, or the Circular Embroidery attachment for perfect circles. Technical adaptability to creative machine stitched sashiko are endless.

Pattern choices are many. Based on geometric shapes, categories are divided into squares, diagonals, diamonds, circles, hexagons and verticals. Each pattern category is arranged from simple to complex, based on the number of stops and starts of individual stitch rows.

THE GRID...SQUARE

Squares are the simplest sashiko stitch form. A classic intersection of vertical and horizontal lines with identified order and simplicity.

Connecting Steps

Commonly referred to as mountains, the pattern is a stair step.
Stitch suggestions:
- Stitch pattern diagonally, 1 down then 1 over, etc.
- Engage needle-down to turn accurate points.
- Minimal thread tails to tie.

Intersect horizontal and vertical lines to form
connected crosses - symbol for the oriental ten(+).
Stitch suggestions:
- Stitch all crosses down, then all crosses from
  left to right.
- Engage needle-down.
- Minimal thread tails to tie.

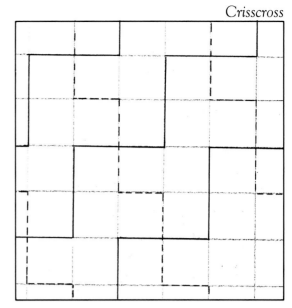

Crisscross

Stitch *Connecting Steps* sequence with
"arrows" in between.
Stitch suggestions:
- Stitch rows of steps in sequence.
- Follow grid arrows to add the short
  diagonal rows of feathers.
- Complete a row of feathers, tie threads;
  repeat sequence for continuous rows.
- Engage needle-down and presser foot lift.
- Alternate thread colors for interesting
  effect.

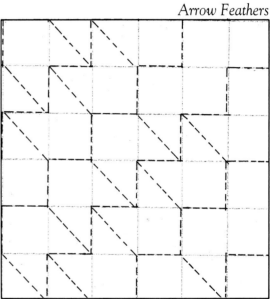

Arrow Feathers

Mark *exact* beginning and end of each
vertical/horizontal line.
Stitch suggestions:
- Stitch vertical rows, then pull threads to
  back and tie.
- Stitch horizontal rows, then pull threads to
  back and tie.
- Utilize Open Embroidery foot for
  maximum visibility.
- Easy marking is implemented with seam
  guide on presser foot.

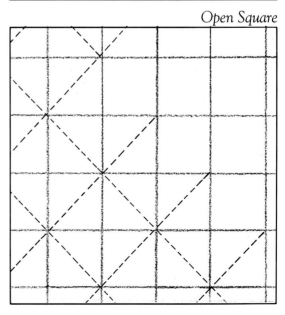

Open Square

Pyramid Square

Connecting steps sewn to center height, then down again.

Stitch suggestions:
- Identify center high point, then begin stitching steps at low side, stitching 1 row up, 1 row across, 1 row up, 1 across, etc. to center, then across 2, down 1, across 1, down 1, etc. until pyramid is completed.
- Repeat on successive rows.
- Engage needle-down and presser foot lift for each pivot.
- Easy, minimum thread tails.

Square Walkway

Interaction of different thread colors makes this pattern interesting.

Stitch suggestions:
- Sew one color across pattern, then change to second color, etc.
- Frequent color change requires thread tying. Keep consistent bobbin thread color.
- Easy to stitch, numerous thread ties.
- Result is visual illusion of walkway.

THE GRID...DIAMOND

Traditionally a square turned on point, of equal sides, or more commonly, one
pair of angles is oblique. Early patterns evolved from a Japanese water chestnut,
whose leaf is an irregular, elongated diamond shape.

Classic Diamond

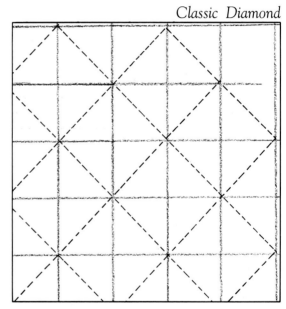

Square shape turned on point.

Stitch suggestions:

- Stitch diagonal rows across points of chalk
  drawn square grid.
- Continuously stitch one row to another.
- Support fabric with a stabilizer to avoid
  stretching bias.
- Easy to sew, minimum tying.

Oblique Diamond

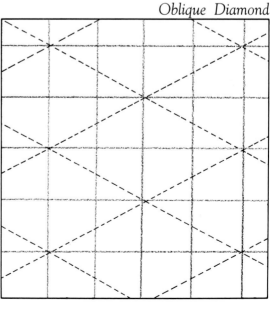

Diagonal lines drawn across 2 squares on grid,
intersecting at every 4th square across and
every 2 down.

Stitch suggestions:

- Stitch diagonally to diamond point, turn
  corner and continue down connecting line.
- Continuously stitch one row to another.
- Stitch on stabilized fabric to avoid
  stretching bias.
- Minimum tying.

41

Diagonal of a Square

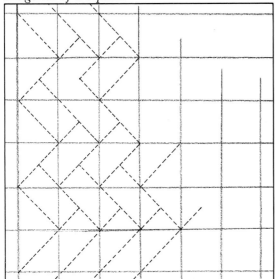

Multi-step zigzag based on traditional fencing.
Stitch suggestions:
- Stitch continuous arched rows in zigzag manner as far as possible.
- Add short rows to complete.
- Pull threads to back and tie.

Woven Bamboo

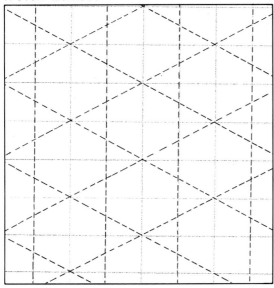

Pattern influenced by traditional bamboo baskets.
Stitch suggestions:
- Stitch vertical rows first.
- Add diagonal rows.
- Simple to sew, minimum tying.

Diamond within Diamond

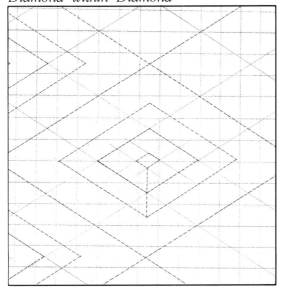

Large diamond is complemented by continuous line square. Stitch suggestions:
- Stitch pattern of diamond rows.
- Add inner diamond squares in one step by stitching out perimeter then diagonal line inward to next row. Repeat to inner dimension.
- Utilize presser foot lifter, needle-down.
- Simple to sew, minimum tying.

Multi-step diamond pattern.

Stitch suggestions:

- Stitch large pattern of diamonds.
- Add "filler" diamonds in matching or contrast thread.
- Utilize presser foot lifter and needle-down.
- Numerous thread tails to tie.

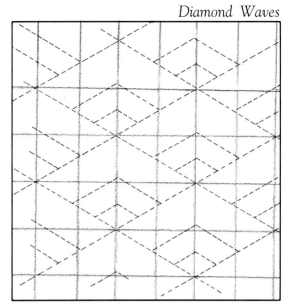

Diamond Waves

Interwoven diagonal strips.

Stitch suggestions:

- Turn square grid on point, then draw grid 4 up, 4 down, counting blocks on grid.
- Stitch a continuous zigzag across rows.
- Fill in short rows last.
- Utilize presser foot lift and needle-down.
- Numerous threads to tie.
- Variations are possible with double thread or thread contrast.

Cypress Fence

43

THE GRID...CURVES

Influenced by round shapes everywhere - waves, flowers, clouds. Easily drawn with circle template placed on top of square grid. Intersect the circle template score lines with the square grid lines, then chalk perfect circle shapes.

Clam Shell

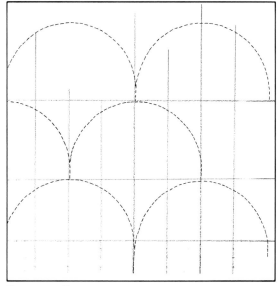

Also called *clam shell* in traditional quilt pattern.
Stitch suggestions:
- Place the circle template even to the two inch square grid.
- Align lower score of circle template to center of next line.
- Draw each circle with chalk pencil.
- Stitch continuously, using needle-down for exact stitch formation.
- Maximum tying.

Pampas Grass

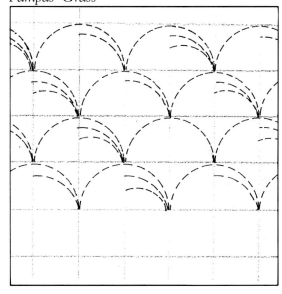

Represents grass blowing in the wind.
Stitch suggestions:
- Repeat clam shell motif.
- Add blades of grass using the same size template to draw short lines.
- Utilize presser foot lifter to move from one short row to another.
- Numerous thread tying.

Other common names include Wedding Ring, Connected Cloisonne and Cathedral Window.

Stitch suggestions:

- Draw serpentine lines of circles by aligning row 1 and 2 exactly under each other.
- Add the interlaced circle by matching the grid to middle of each set circles.
- Sew serpentine lines, stitching left and right across curve. Stitch as far as possible in one direction, then turn around at end of pattern and stitch opposite serpentine.
- Fill in the *short* circle units as necessary.
- Numerous thread ties.

Seven Treasures of Budda

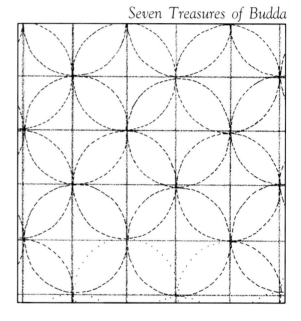

THE GRID...OGEE NETWORK

Based on the S curve, the design involves both concave and convex contours. Historically influenced by vines, stems, and tendrils placed on a gridded network. Variety is achieved by overlapping the serpentine movement.

Counterweights

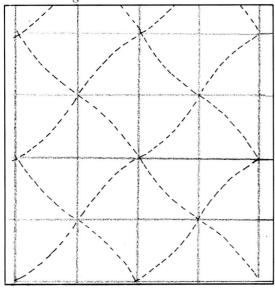

Based on shape of weight used by Japanese on traditional scales.

Stitch suggestions:

- Place circle template to upper left corner of one inch scale, then lower left corner. Draw design across first row.
- Place circle template to upper right corner, then lower right corner. Draw design across second row.
- Stitch curve continuously in serpentine fashion to one end. Turn cloth with presser foot lift and continue stitching.
- Easy to sew, few threads to tie.

The Net

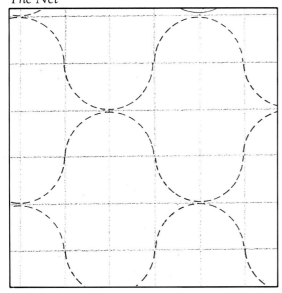

Taken from the fishing net, it is a serpentine formed by alternating the top and bottom half of a circle on a square grid.

Stitch suggestions:

- With circle template, draw circle up, then down across two inch horizontal grid.
- Alternate next horizontal row by drawing circle down, then up across two inch grid.
- Easy to stitch, few threads to tie.

THE GRID...HEXAGON

Tortoise shells and honeycombs are examples of nature's hexagon. The hexagon is a radius of a circle divided into six equal points. It was first recorded in the ancient civilization of west Asia.

Hemp Leaf

Six-sided star pattern. Draw in three steps.

Stitch suggestions:

- Draw equilateral triangles.
- Add short parallel diagonal lines.
- Last, add short vertical segment.
- Complex to draw and stitch.
- Sew in the continuous line technique.
- Utilize presser foot lift and needle-down.
- Numerous threads to tie.

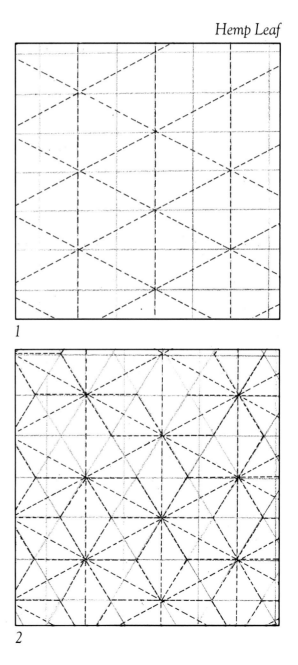

1

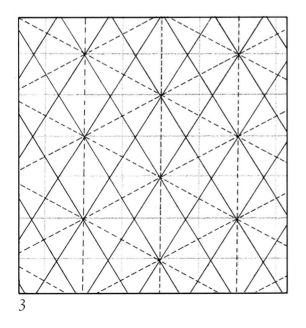

3

2

THE GRID...LINES...STRAIGHT OR CURVED

Visually seen as stripes, checks or plaids, the vertical and horizontal lines create calmness or energy as they are sewn in variable distance from each other.

Arrows

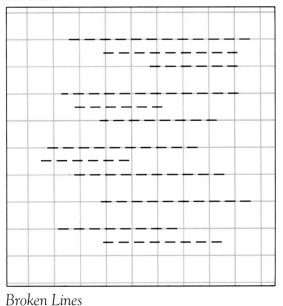

Short darts placed equally from each other.
Stitch suggestions:
- Draw chalk lines in broken arrangements of three across fabric.
- Stitch a line, then using presser foot lifter, move to next location.
- Cut thread tails at each group of three, pull to back and tie.
- Easy to sew, numerous ties.

Broken Lines

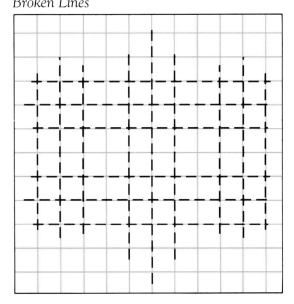

Short thread units of even length, can be aligned vertically or horizontally.
Stitch suggestions:
- Stitch unit, then with presser foot lifter, slide to next line.
- Cut thread tails, pull behind and tie.

Sashiko - Expanding the Beginning or Variations on the Grid

Novelty designing with traditional sashiko grids is unlimited when machine decorative stitches and accessories are combined with innovative pattern and thread choices.

From the basics of the classic running stitch, try grids with multiple stitch combinations. Alter traditional patterns with a decorative pattern every other row, or combine two stitches in memory. The result of a straight stitch turning into a zigzag is spontaneous, yet stitched row after row, reinforces the dignity and beauty of sashiko patterns.

With the vast array of threads available in the marketplace, sashiko also adapts to different moods. Look for unusual threads such as metallic and rayon, cotton and blends, and experiment with traditional patterns. Multiple appearances are possible with a simple choice of thread and fabric. Each pattern can evolve into dressy or casual, traditional or non-traditional by stitching the patterns in threads customized to the project.

Endless options for variety are available in sashiko combinations. Motifs gain strength and boundaries when combined with grid patterns. Traditional patterns stitched with a decorative machine stitch are interesting alone, or sewn in a series of designs. For example, try zigzag stitches every other row of a traditional pattern. Or try the serpentine running stitch sewn row after row. It doesn't have to match and is often more interesting if each row falls to a slightly different curve.

Review the different styles of classic decorative machine stitches drawn on the front of the machine. They are identified in the machine manual as zigzag, serpentine, honeycomb or feather and look beautiful adapted into sashiko designs. Fuller stitches, referred to as compact patterns are also successful. Most decorative stitches are easily stitched in sashiko patterns by simply increasing the stitch length of the pattern. The increased stitch length balances to thicker novelty threads and complements the traditional running stitch appearance.

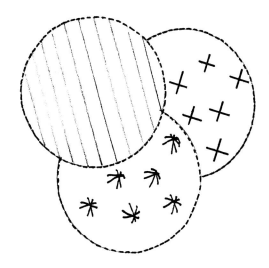

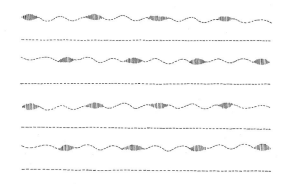

Another successful stitch option for sashiko patterns is a combination of stitches sewn in a series. The memory capacity of the modern computer machine is designed to recall stitches in a sequenced order. Bernina's memory is easy to operate and records stitch units from five to 50 or more. To create a calm, but interesting repetition sew a series of straight stitches between a zigzag or honeycomb stitch series. This combination is particularly strong on borders or adjacent to a busy pattern such as *Seven Treasures of Budda.*

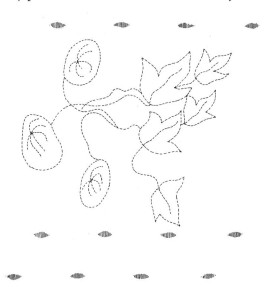

It also is an attractive background stitch used throughout a series of sashiko patterns. For example, all vertical rows of a pattern might adapt to a sequenced pattern, while horizontal rows maintain the traditional straight running stitch.

Try these specific expanded memory patterns in selected rows of sashiko grid patterns:

1. Five zigzag stitches (stitch width 5, stitch length 4) with five straight stitches (stitch length 4).
2. Four honeycomb stitches (stitch width 5, stitch length 3) with five straight stitches (stitch length 4).
3. Five serpentine stitches (stitch width 5, stitch length 4) with one compact oval stitch (stitch length 4).
4. The straight stitch in memory is equal to one grid measurement. Utilize needle-down on machine, pivot, then repeat memory length of straight stitch, pivot, etc. The machine will sew the same distance again and again - great for exact grid stitches.
5. Alphabet with straight stitches - spell a name, an event and join with a series of straight stitches. Stitch a sashiko pattern with name repetition, simply repeated in computerized memory.

MOTIFS AND TRADITIONAL SYMBOLS

Symbols are strong visual components of sashiko. The fan, birds, contrast borders and expanded pattern imagery are often stitched in sashiko. Each of these are easy to sew with the guidelines below.

FAN

Historical records indicate Japan invented the folding fan about 700 A.D. It became a favorite symbol of beauty, with very decorative art pieces designed for the wealthy. Early sashiko work combines fans with grids and favorite motifs.

To Stitch a Fan

1. Draw the curve of
a fan in a corner
between two grid
patterns. Fans are
typically more
attractive stitched
in a lower corner

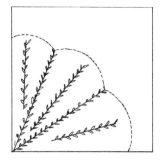

with the spokes worked upward. Then
machine stitch the outer edge with:

   a. the scallop stitch in single or double
   rows. Utilize the *pattern begin* function
   button to match each row of pattern to
   first.

   b. wide zigzag around the outer fan edge.

   c. two or more thread colors stitched
   adjacent to each other.

   d. one straight row around outer edge,
   complemented by decorative stitches
   above it. If sewn with heavier thread,
   always increase stitch length.

2. Sew spokes of fan from wide to narrow,
leaving thread tails on outside of fabric.
Tails look attractive hanging freely, or with
small beads tied at ends.

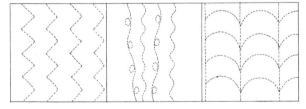

Double Pattern

Computerized machines have an option of
increasing pattern size while maintaining stitch
shape. Utilize this attractive function to design
single patterns of flower centers or try circle
designs combined to a straight stitch. The
circle expands to an oval style and is handsome
in mirror image, combined with a straight
stitch. The machine memory reversed the
circle from the left to right side of the straight
stitch series.

Circular Embroidery Attachment

Frame a design in a
circle motif with a
diameter from two to 14
inches. All machine
stitches can be sewn in a
perfect circle. The diameter
can be decreased or increased by
a simple adjustment on the
accessory bar. Multiple borders
can be stitched by increasing the
size of circle.

Some circle options are:

1. Satin Stitch Edging - Stitch a perfect circle
of satin stitch around a motif/grid design. It
frames the sashiko pattern and is a strong
format for pillow centers, table linens, etc.

2. Alphabet Edging - The alphabet can be
programmed to stitch words in a circle to
complement the sashiko pattern within.
Pattern names stitched around the grid
pattern become an interesting variation
and lend strength and originality to a
typical pattern.

3. Decorative Stitch Edging - Select a
decorative stitch suited to the sashiko
design. Place the fabric on the pin equal to
desired circle size. Repeat in multiple rows,
by increasing gauge on Circular
Embroidery attachment.

ANIMAL AND FLORAL MOTIFS

Popular motifs of animals and flowers are
available from numerous resources. Review
favorite botanical and wildlife books,
children's coloring books, and wallpaper or
home decor resources. Trace the design on
plain paper, then needle-punch perforations
on design lines (refer to Chapter 4). Mount
paper design to fabric and pounce powder
through perforations. Remove paper and
chalk design to fabric, tracing the powder
dots.

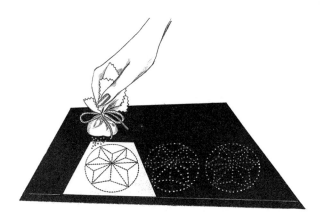

Stitch motif designs with an Open Embroidery foot, feed-dogs up, if the design is simple. If the design is complex with many turns, it is more easily stitched with the Freehand Embroidery foot and the feed-dogs lowered.

A selection of numerous machine patterns and computer functions is fun to try and often lends strength to the variety of traditional grids and motifs. A primary visual focus of sashiko is the beauty of numerous patterns stitched adjacent to another. Each is stronger, worked in multiple rows. Assorted threads and modern machine functions are merely opportunities to enhance the traditional stitch.

CHAPTER 8

The Projects

Sashiko patterns are beautiful in their simplicity. The running stitch has a captivating charm about it as it meanders across cloth in rows to become rails and bricks, or in angular repetition, forming one hemp leaf after another. It is a natural stitch technique for embellishment of clothing, accessories and home dec projects. Each sashiko design by machine lends beauty, durability and variety to home and personal crafts.

The focus of information for each of the classic projects discussed in this chapter is supplies, machine stitching, and general construction techniques. Finishing tips are given in Chapter 9. Sashiko embellishment on the different projects can range from one simple sashiko motif such as a crest, to an elaborate rendition of multiple designs worked together, as in the featured coat. It is hoped the variation will be helpful in planning personal projects.

Because commercial pattern styles quickly become outdated by pattern companies, specific pattern numbers are not given. Instead, projects are featured with classical styling. Refer to each project as general style, adapting fabric suggestions and specific suggestions for machine stitched details to similar commercial patterns, or perhaps a totally different project.

Plan each sashiko embellished project with quality materials, appropriate battings, linings and finishing details. It will be worth the extra time and money spent to select fabrics and threads that reinforce quality and fashion equal to the time represented.

CLOTHING PROJECTS

Sashiko stitching is a perfect way to lend an accent detail to otherwise mundane clothing. Select clothing styles that are uncluttered (free of multiple seams, darts, insets, etc.) and lend to sashiko embellishment. Vests and cardigan style jackets are particularly adaptable to sashiko stitching.

The clothing projects in this chapter are sashiko designed in a different sewing technique, ranging from a heavy thread (cordonnet) sewn in the needle to ribbon-like threads, bobbin stitched to the fabric. Designs are both traditional and non-traditional sashiko patterns.

The DENIM VEST…is designed with assorted sashiko patterned squares patch-worked over a muslin base. Each square is sashiko stitched individually, then stitched to a backing fabric.

The RED SILK NOIL VEST…is sashiko stitched in the bobbin thread technique, stitched from a pattern traced on the underside of the fabric.

The GREEN SILK JACKET…takes a different stitch approach with American patchwork design worked in the sashiko stitch technique. Different thread colors identify interrelated pattern units.

And last, the DENIM COAT…is a crowned love affair of sashiko. The traditional folkwear pattern interrelates grid and motif designs, and intersects them one to another, pattern after pattern. It is a sashiko classic - a coat to wear forever.

TO BEGIN…MAKE A SAMPLE

To plan a new sashiko garment, first make a sample of the basic pattern shape in muslin. Simply cut front, back and sleeves (facings and collars are not necessary) in muslin and stitch the basic line. Try the muslin shell on and evaluate the ease, flare, sleeve length and general appearance. Make adjustments if necessary. If the pattern choice isn't workable, much time has been saved and another pattern can be considered. When pattern fitting details are worked out, plan the sashiko embellishment.

An easy way to plot the sashiko designs across a garment is on paper, prior to developing it on cloth. If the pattern is commercial, select the silhouette shapes of the major pieces from the guide sheet, then pull the front and back tissue pattern pieces from the envelope. Press, then place the tissue pattern pieces on large sheets of paper with the side seams overlapped. Large sheets of mailing paper work nicely for drawing paper. Trace around the cutting edges of each pattern front and back, then tuck tissue pattern back in envelope. Next, draw lines across paper pattern to indicate placement of different sashiko designs. Grid each of these sections into one inch lines. Draw or plan specific sashiko grid patterns in each space.

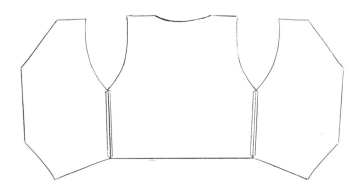

Plan a simple motif in only one garment area, or design sashiko stitching across the total garment. Stitches can be sewn repetitively in only one pattern, or they can be patchworked in multiple patterns across the garment shape. For maximum beauty, layout the designs carefully at center front (match stitch lines from left to right), and with complementary sleeves and side seams.

ADD UNDERLINING, INTERFACING OR BATTING

Sashiko embellished wearables are more beautiful and durable when stitched with a support fabric (flannelette), interfacing or batting underneath. The support fabric gives body to the garment and hides tied sashiko thread tails on the underside. If a lighter weight garment is desired, add support fabric, such as muslin or lightweight fusible interfacing under the sashiko stitched area. If warmth is desired for a total garment, insert flannelette or low-loft batting under each front and back garment piece. If designed as an outer wear garment, also insert the warm support fabrics in the sleeves.

STEP BY STEP...GENERAL CLOTHING CONSTRUCTION GUIDELINES

1) Cut a rectangular shaped (slightly longer than pattern piece) outer fabric for each garment front, back and sleeve. Cut the same size rectangular support fabric (muslin, fusible knit tricot interfacing* or low-loft batting) for each piece.

   * If fusible knit tricot interfacing is choice, fuse it to the wrong side of fabric piece prior to chalk marking grid or motif on fabric.

2) Trace around pattern shape on each fabric piece with chalk marker. Chalk sashiko design lines in grid or motif pattern to each piece. Refer to paper sketch.

3) If appropriate to project, pin support fabrics (muslin, flannelette or low-loft batting) under outer fabric.

4) Set up machine with chosen thread and needle, stitch pattern, width and length.

5) Stitch sashiko patterns according to drawings and guidelines given with each project.

6) Finish garment as pattern suggests with facings, linings, etc.

PATCHWORK DENIM VEST

This classic vest style is a good project for a sampling of fabrics and sashiko designs worked collectively. Assemble the following supplies and begin.

SUPPLIES:

Classic vest pattern

7-8 pieces of fabric - each approximately six inch square. Select medium weight, different dark colored fabrics in textures such as linen, corduroy, denim, and bottom-weight cotton/support fabrics, as necessary.

One yard muslin backing for vest fronts

Vest back yardage - to pattern requirements

Vest lining - to pattern requirements

Small stripe or printed cotton for bias strips - 1/2 yard

Cordonnet thread - white and red

Sashiko stitch patterns of choice (Chapter 6)
General sewing supplies
Chalk marker and ruler, pouncer
Special accessories: Open Embroidery foot,
   Edge Stitch foot

DIRECTIONS:

1) Transfer grid or motif markings to individually supported fabric squares and stitch different sashiko designs on each fabric. As necessary, pull sashiko thread tails to back and tie.

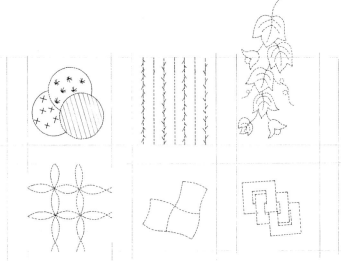

Machine Hint: Sew with a longer stitch length and the Open Embroidery foot. The foot provides visibility to every stitch.

2) Finish and press each designed patch, wrong side up. Set aside.

3) Trace vest or jacket front shapes to muslin.

4) Arrange designed patches on muslin fronts in random fashion, working from top downward. Pin each square in place, arranging the sashiko stitched patterns to flow attractively from side to side and completely fill the muslin background.

   Hint: In patchwork arrangement, consider buttonhole placement and avoid placing intricately stitched sashiko at those markings.

5) Bias strips are ideal to finish the cut edges between the sashiko stitched squares. Cut bias strips (Chapter 9). Fold bias strip in half, aligning cut edges together. Pin bias edges to cut edges of sashiko squares. Stitch 1/4 inch seam. Turn folded edge over the stitched seam and edge stitch with foot #10. The Edge Stitch foot guides the stitch line for perfectly straight stitching.

6) Pin vest tissue pattern fronts over embellished yardage. Trim excess sashiko fabric and muslin to the pattern shape.

7) Complete vest to pattern directions.

RED SILK NOIL VEST

Floral designs are favorite sashiko patterns and have been recorded since ancient times. A simple and beautiful alternate sashiko stitch method of stitching floral or other motifs is with thread sewn from the bobbin. So many beautiful ribbon-like threads are available in today's market, it is an ideal choice with many colors. The heavier thread sewn from bobbin, increases motif visibility and impact.

Two readily available threads, rayon pearl and ribbon thread, are easy to sew when filled on a bobbin, then sewn as a bobbin thread. An advantage of stitching the motifs from the bobbin thread is the option of drawing the pattern exactly on the under side of the support fabric. The design is finished as the needle goes around the pattern, right side of fabric face down on the sewing machine table.

Begin the red vest by assembling fabric and supplies.

SUPPLIES:

    Classic vest pattern
    Decorative outer yardage (silk noil)
    Muslin for pattern drawing and support
    Vest back and lining
    Threads:
        pearl rayon/ for bobbin
        ribbon floss/ for bobbin
        metallic top thread
        polyester top thread
    General sewing supplies
    Chalk marker and ruler, pouncer
    Glass seed beads
    Special accessories: Black latch bobbin case, Freehand Embroidery foot

DIRECTIONS:

1) Cut rectangular units of vest yardage in muslin and outer fabric. Trace vest shape of pattern pieces to muslin. Transfer sashiko motifs to muslin with pouncer

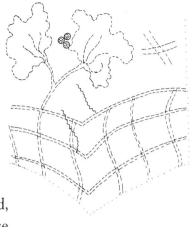

method (refer to Chapter 2).

2) Thread bobbin with selected ornamental thread (Chapter 3). Insert bobbin in Black latch bobbin case. Thread needle with polyester thread, matching color. Place Freehand Embroidery foot on machine.

3) Pin muslin and outer fabric fronts together (muslin to wrong side of outer fabric).

4) Place vest front fabric right side down, under machine presser foot. Drop feed-dogs. Begin stitching by moving fabric slowly and sewing with even, moderate speed. Stitch as far as possible in a continuous mode. When design motif is finished, stop leaving a short (about four inches) tail of thread. Pull thread to back of garment with a hand darning needle; tie snug to fabric, trim thread tail.

Try these techniques to achieve finished look:

5) Stitch second row adjacent to first, to achieve double rows of checkerboard squares.

6) Add motif details including stylized grid designs and a solid bud motif. Stitch designs as below, with bobbin thread in free-motion technique. Arrange design placement randomly on vest fronts. Decorative stitches are also stitched on vest. The feather stitch is attractive sewn in metallic thread.

7) To create dimension in the floral motifs, stitch a different thread color and texture (i.e., metallic) next to portions of the bobbin thread. Lightweight threads are sewn from the top with polyester on

bobbin. Add decorative machine feather stitch at random locations.

8) After motif stitching is completed, trim vest shape from tissue pattern, and construct garment according to pattern instructions.

GREEN SILK JACKET

Occasionally a pattern idea takes a different turn than the classic sashiko patterns. The sashiko stitches (the classic running stitch) are not limited only to Japanese influenced design; the stitch technique also transfers to assorted motifs from any society. One American favorite, the patchwork pattern, is such as example. The patterns on this jacket are stitch interpretations of popular patchwork motifs with names like *Jacob's Ladder*, *4-Patch*, *Goose Chase*, etc. Try this variation, and remember, let patchwork influence sashiko, with a

change of thread color in the middle of the pattern blocks, or at the turn of an edge. The change of thread colors represent the assorted patchwork shapes.

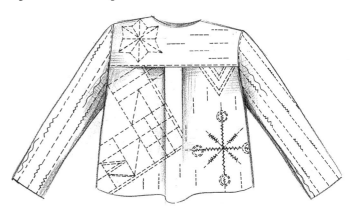

SUPPLIES:

   Unstructured jacket pattern (Chanel styling)
   Jacket fabric, muslin backing, lining fabric
   Favorite patchwork patterns
   Multi-colors of cordonnet thread
   General sewing notions
   Chalk marker and ruler
   Special accessory: Open Embroidery foot

DIRECTIONS:

1) Plan patterns across jacket fronts and back. If necessary, refer to general directions.

2) Select support fabrics, fuse if necessary. Chalk patchwork designs across fabric.

3) Pin muslin under jacket fabric shapes. Begin stitching patchwork pattern motifs across jacket units, changing thread colors as often as desired. Each time a thread color is stopped, pull the thread tail to underside and tie. Start new thread color by inserting new needle thread color exactly into row of last stitch. Begin and end each color by pulling a tail of thread to to the back when stitching is finished. The thread stitch rows appear continuous and have stronger beauty.

   Hint: Develop uniqueness and interest in the sashiko patchwork patterns by utilizing the machine's computer/memory function. Select 2-3 stitches to be stitched in a continuous row. Adjust stitch width and length to desired look, insert into memory, then sew continuous rows. One of the most attractive stitch units is a zigzag/straight stitch worked in straight rows equal distance apart (see Variations, Chapter 7). Use the stitch pattern down the sleeve or in continuous rows of repetitive design. Complete sashiko/patchwork patterns across jacket fronts, back and sleeves.

4) Finish jacket according to pattern directions.

ALL-WEATHER COAT

An all-weather coat of denim becomes a classic of sashiko design when a variety of sashiko stitches embellish individual panels. Styled with stitch lines dividing each coat panel, different sashiko patterns are worked in blocks, and matched from left to right. Grid patterns are sewn in the vertical panels, with motif shapes accenting the hem and waistline. Channel quilting reinforces the facing edges. A project such as the sashiko coat is worth the time invested, as it can be utilized for years on end. Begin with an understated coat style that fits nicely (refer to General Clothing Guidelines). Select a set of coordinated threads (about five colors) that can be stitched in assorted mixtures from pattern to pattern. Begin with a selection of fabric and thread.

SUPPLIES:

    Coat pattern (classic with minimum details)
    Denim yardage for coat
    Low-loft quilt batting
    Lining yardage
    Cordonnet threads (about five in
      coordinated colors; amount of thread

varies to project, but allow ample)
General sewing supplies
Chalk marker and ruler, pouncer
Special accessory: Open Embroidery foot

DIRECTIONS:

1) Cut rectangle shapes of denim and low-loft quilt batting for each section (fronts, back, side-pieces, sleeves). If desired, fuse knit-tricot interfacing to underside of denim to prevent fabric stretching.

2) Chalk primary divisions of sashiko patterns to the coat units, matching seams of center front, sides and back. Chalk sashiko designs in a single section at a time. The chalk has a tendency to come off, therefore, it is wasted effort to chalk an entire section at once. Place low-loft batting under the denim shapes. Stitch sashiko designs through denim/batting thickness. Stitch patterns in continuous quilt pattern technique, then pull sashiko threads to back and tie as necessary.

3) Change thread colors in and among the patterns. It is also effective to work a continuous sashiko vertical stitch down coat units to create a background of pattern. The straight/zigzag (see Variations, Chapter 7) pattern is a good design choice.

4) Stitch and finish sashiko designs across every denim shape. Stitch sashiko motif designs in center back and hemline section. Repeat some stitch rows with adjacent coordinated colors to increase motif design strength.

5) Place pattern piece over the sashiko stitched denim and cut fronts, back, side

and sleeve units.

6) Finish coat construction according to pattern guide sheet. Stitch a coat label (see Chapter 9) and sew to top center back of lining. Insert lining. Finish coat by topstitching continuous rows of channel quilting along facing edges.

TOTES

Totes are convenient to carry everything from books to lunches. The rectangle shape adapts to many variations of sashiko design and the stitching lends itself to an attractive border or over-all design. A sashiko trimmed tote is simple to design, yet changes the ordinary into the special. Make each style with different sasiko designs.

Sashiko Pocket on Tote

Select a tote pattern that has a rectangle strip sewn across the lower front and back and becomes a pocket when the straps are added. Divide the pocket strip into equal widths and stitch a different sashiko pattern in each panel.

SUPPLIES:

> Tote pattern
> Notions as suggested by pattern
> Denim yardage for bag
> Fusible interfacing for sashiko stitched
>   fabric
> Low-loft quilt batting
> Lining yardage
> Cordonnet thread
> General sewing supplies
> Chalk marker and ruler, pouncer
> Special accessory: Open Embroidery foot

DIRECTIONS:

1) Cut outer fabric, batting and lining by tote pattern. Fuse interfacing to tote pocket strip.

2) Divide the pocket strip into equal widths; chalk grid design on each section. Following grid lines stitch a different sashiko pattern in each panel.

3) Secure pocket strip to bag at lower center of front and back. Make straps for front and back of bag.

4) Add straps, stitch sides closed and insert lining.

Sashiko Patterned Fabric on Large Tote

With the memory capacity of the computerized machine it is fun to design custom sashiko fabric. Patterns can be designed singularly, or sewn in a continuous series. The gold stitched tote was stitched with memory patterns in gold thread on denim fabric. Computerized pattern options include single pattern (stitches one pattern), and continuous patterns (stitches several patterns in sequence). A free motion floral motif completes the design.

If the tote pattern style is divided into two or more pattern pieces, select one section for the single motif and the other section for continuous vertical patterns. Plan the single motifs in random arrangement or draw a grid line on cloth for a uniform arrangement. Continuous pattern arrangement is most pleasing with two to three designs worked in vertical rows. Consider the serpentine stitch with a closely spaced stitch. Program the machine to repeat stitch the serpentine five to six stitches, then one of the closely spaced stitches.

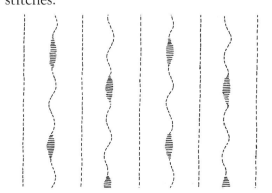

Hint: To sew closely spaced stitches with cordonnet, increase stitch length slightly.

Tote pattern
Notions suggested by pattern
Denim yardage for bag
Low-loft quilt batting
Lining yardage
Cordonnet thread
General sewing supplies
Chalk marker and ruler, pouncer
Special accessories: Open Embroidery foot,
    Freehand Embroidery foot

DIRECTIONS:

1) Cut outer fabric, batting and lining by tote pattern. Fuse interfacing to tote fabric shapes.

2) Place batting under tote fabric shapes. Select and record in memory a single pattern. Remember to slightly increase stitch length. Stitch the single pattern randomly across upper half of tote front and back.

3) To sashiko embellish the lower half of tote front and back, change the stitch memory to a continuous arrangement of two to three designs. Draw a grid on the denim, then sew the repeated design across the yardage, creating a striped effect.

   Hint: Utilize the seam guide on back of sewing foot for accurate repetitive rows.

4) To stitch the floral motif on bag, pounce design on fabric. With the Freehand Embroidery foot, stitch the design in continuous line direction. When necessary to stop stitch row, leave a tail of thread. Pull to back and tie.

5) Join the top and bottom units together for front and back of tote. Join side seams and add straps. Insert lining.

The Draw-string Tote

Add the classic draw-string bag to the tote collection, as the vertical shape easily goes to the beach, the library or a casual dinner. The bag is adaptable to many looks, from batik stitched with sashiko to denim, as featured. Denim is durable and resists stains, while the sashiko stitches, worked in sampler style, add a personal touch.

Many draw-string bags are available in pattern books. Select one large enough to add a sashiko accented pocket along the lower edge . The pocket is a rectangle of denim, folded in half for stability and attractiveness. Sashiko stitches are sewn in equal divisions along the panel creating a sampler of favorite patterns.

SUPPLIES:

Draw-string tote pattern
Denim yardage for bag
Fusible interfacing for bag shaping
Five inch square fleece/bottom support
Lining
Approximately three yards pull cord (strap)
Cordonnet thread
General sewing supplies
Chalk marker and ruler
Special accessory: Open Embroidery foot

DIRECTIONS:

1) Cut outer fabric, batting and lining by tote pattern. Fuse interfacing to individual pattern pieces.

2) To make the sashiko panel around lower edge of tote, cut a rectangular denim strip for front and back (approximately 13 inches high X tote width). Interface (fusible tricot) the sashiko panel, then press in half.

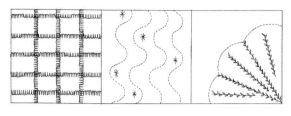

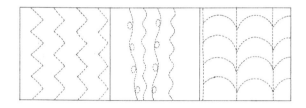

3) Chalk grid the panel below the crease, then stitch favorite sashiko patterns across the panel through single thickness.

4) Fold fabric in half, showing pattern on the front side. Stitch the sashiko panel to primary tote fabric, attaching the decorated panel to tote with vertical lines of stitching between each pattern.

5) Finish tote according to pattern directions.

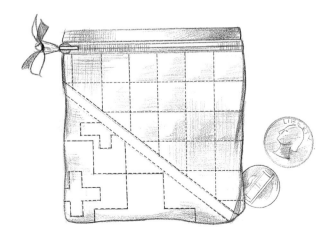

Cosmetic Bag

Virtually any size of bag can be constructed with sashiko designs. The small cosmetic bags are ideal because they are easy to stitch and make great gifts. Assemble small pieces of fabric, zippers and sashiko designs.

SUPPLIES:

Assorted rectangular pieces of denim, low-loft batting and lining

Matching zipper for horizontal width of each bag

Cordonnet thread

Sashiko patterns

General sewing supplies

Chalk marker and ruler

Special accessories: Open Embroidery foot, Zipper foot with guide

DIRECTIONS:

1) Cut and support denim rectangles as desired (fusible interfacing, muslin, low-loft batting).

2) Draw sashiko grid on each bag.

3) Stitch sashiko design on each rectangular shape of denim and batting.

4) Insert zipper in horizontal width of rectangle.

5) Fold up sides and stitch.

6) Construct lining of rectangle shape, same size as denim. Stitch horizontal edges to zipper edge. Stitch up side seams, right sides together and slightly narrower. Turn into cosmetic bag.

HOME DEC ACCENTS

One of the nicest aspects of sashiko by machine is the stitch beauty incorporated into most home dec looks. A change of thread texture or color, a change of fabric, and the stitch designs transform a room decor. Consider pillows, table toppers and place mats for your home.

Pillow Squares Inset with Sashiko

Construct a great pillow with 12 inch squares of your favorite sashiko design, then border with fabrics to match your room decor. Add a colored strip of a room accent color between the sashiko and border fabric. Coordinate threads, background fabric and home dec fabric for a special accent.

SUPPLIES:

13 inch square of denim for sashiko
13 inch tear-away or other support yardage
One yard border and pillow backing fabric
1/4 yard inset contrast color strip
Pillow form - size of choice
Cordonnet thread
General sewing supplies
Chalk marker and ruler
Special accessory: Freehand Embroidery foot

DIRECTIONS:

1) Draw sashiko grid on denim fabric. Place tear-away or other support under fabric, then sew selected sashiko pattern.

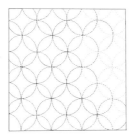

Consider accenting intersections of the sashiko design with a *single pattern* from the decorative machine stitches.

2) Cut border strips, pillow backing and accent color strips.

3) Square the sashiko stitched fabric, to an equal width on all sides. Trim edges, as necessary. Fold one inch color accent strips in half and press. Place cut edge of folded strip to each cut edge of sashiko square. Stitch accent strips to sashiko fabric with a 1/4 inch seam, creating a 1/4 inch border of color.

4) Place border strips even to cut edge of accented sashiko. Add each strip, first stitching top and bottom strips, then adding the left and right sides. Press seams flat as you work.

5) Place front and back pillow pieces right sides together. Sew 1/2 inch seam around all edges leaving a small opening on one side. If desired, sew Turkish corners (see Finishing Touches, Chapter 9) for a unique look.

6) Turn pillow unit right side out. Insert pillow form. Stitch lower edge closed.

Pillow Squares Inset with Circled Sashiko

Occasionally it is enjoyable to utilize several sewing techniques in one project. This pillow design combines the Circular Embroidery attachment, grid and motif sashiko, and simple thread embellishment on pillow fabric. Assemble a beautiful solid color fabric for center with a heavy textured fabric for the borders. Select an accent print for the piping.

SUPPLIES:

    13 inch square of bottom weight cotton fabric (for sashiko stitching)

    13 inch square tear-away or other support yardage

    One yard for pillow borders and back

    1/2 yard for gathered piping

    1/2 inch cotton piping X perimeter of pillow

    Cordonnet thread

    One skein embroidery floss

    Pillow form - size of choice

    Chalk marker and ruler

    Special accessories: Circular Embroidery attachment, Open Embroidery foot, Freehand Embroidery foot, Leather roller foot

DIRECTIONS:

1) Pounce and draw sashiko design on chosen center fabric.

    a) Stitch motif with the Freehand Embroidery foot. Work details of fins, etc., stitching one, then another.

        Hint: Secure threads at beginning and end of each stitch unit by stitching in same stitch hole twice.

    b) Change to the Open Embroidery foot and sew the sashiko grid on pillow.

    c) Change to the Circular Embroidery attachment and sew satin stitch (width about 2 1/2) around the sashiko design.

    d) Change to the Freehand Embroidery foot #24 and stitch embroidery floss lengths across yardage. Stitch in the "middle" of a two inch length of floss. Set the zigzag *exactly the width of floss* and set needle into thread unit. This secures the thread to fabric and creates an interesting dimensional fabric, with thread tails randomly placed.

2) Align, then stitch pillow borders to sashiko designed fabric. Stitch top and bottom borders, then side borders. Press the pillow top with sashiko stitching facing down.

3) Make gathered piping for pillow (see Finishing Touches, Chapter 9).

4) Place seam edge of piping to seam edge of pillow front. Stitch piping to pillow. Place back of pillow to front, right sides together, piping sandwiched between. Stitch units together with opening for pillow form. Turn right side out, insert pillow form. Stitch the lower edge closed.

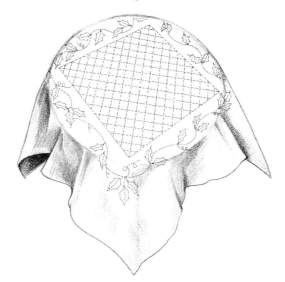

Turquoise Tablecloth Topper

    A table topper is an ideal accent cloth. Cut square, the width of the yardage, it is attractive used alone or over a full size cloth as an accent. Select a beautifully colored fabric and design a sashiko center for a festive look.

SUPPLIES:

    One square yardage (45 x 45)
    1/2 yard iron-on fusible tear-away
    Cordonnet thread
    General sewing supplies
    Chalk marker and ruler, pouncer
    Special accessories: Open Embroidery foot,
        Freehand Embroidery foot

DIRECTIONS:

1) Draw grid square in center of table topper.
Place tear-away stabilizer under design in
center of cloth.

2) Stitch sashiko pattern of choice in center
of cloth, stitching in
continuous
direction. Pull
threads behind and tie.

3) Pounce motif border
pattern around sashiko
grid. With Freehand
Embroidery foot #24
stitch leaves, tendrils and veining of leaves.
There are numerous "stops and starts." Pull
threads to underside and tie.

4) Finish the outer edge of cloth, turn hem
edge under with mitered corners (see
Finishing Touches, Chapter 9) and
machine hem.

Place Mats

    Special table settings create a cordial
atmosphere at the dinner table. Select small
scale patchwork patterns and sashiko stitch as
place mat borders.

SUPPLIES:

    Place mat yardage and lining
    Interfacing or low-loft quilt batting
    Cordonnet thread to match project
    General sewing supplies
    Chalk marker and ruler
    Special accessory: Open Embroidery foot

DIRECTIONS:

1) Cut place mat rectangular shapes of
yardage and lining.

2) Fuse interfacing to underside of each
yardage shape.

3) Chalk sashiko design on corner of each
place mat.

4) Stitch patchwork sashiko design in
continuous stitchery technique, through
interfaced yardage, or, if desired, add the
low-loft batting for a softer place mat. Some
patterns have numerous "stops and starts";
pull threads to underside and tie, as
necessary.

5) Place lining to mat, right sides together. Sew
around edges, leaving an opening to pull
right side out. Turn design outward, smooth
and press edges. Topstitch edge, if desired.

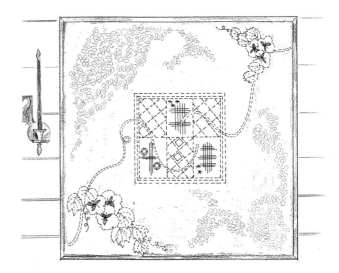

Wall Quilt

    A wall quilt (35" square) shows off the
best of traditional quilting and sashiko

stitches. Select denim yardage for the whole cloth quilt, then stitch the center medallion in different styles of sashiko stitches. Meander tone-on-tone machine quilting around the center for a subtle framework.

SUPPLIES:

One square of denim (35" x 35")
One square of tricot fusible interfacing
    (35" x 35")
One square of printed cotton (35" x 35")
One square of low-loft quilt batting
    (35" x 35")
One yard denim (binding)
All purpose sewing thread
Cordonnet thread
50 wgt. cotton thread
General sewing supplies
Chalk marker and ruler, pouncer
Sashiko patterns for grid and motif designs
Special accessories: Open Embroidery foot,
    Freehand Embroidery foot, Walking foot

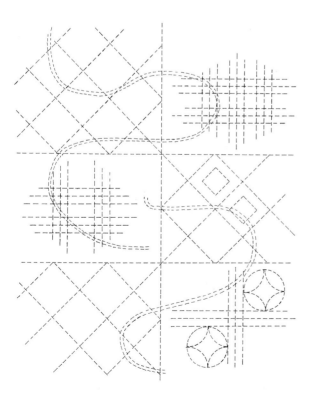

DIRECTIONS:

1) Square yardage for top and lining.
2) Fuse tricot interfacing to underside of denim square.
3) Chalk medallion on center of denim quilt top (see Chapter 4).

> Hint: Tape yardage to a square grid mat. It is easier to draw the center square and floral motif when fabric is taut. If fabric stretching (while drawing) is a problem, slide a light grade sandpaper sheet under the fabric design area. It secures the fabric as the chalk and ruler are slid along to make design.

4) Once the sashiko design is stitched, it is now time to prepare the fabric for quilting. Place the cotton lining on a large flat surface.

5) Smooth batting evenly across the cotton lining.
6) Smooth sashiko stitched denim across the bat and lining.
7) Safety-pin baste the three layers together, pinning the thicknesses together every six inches.
8) With tone-on-tone thread stitch around each rectangle of center medallion (in-the-ditch), adjacent to the sashiko thread patterns. Stitch with the Walking foot to keep all thicknesses smooth and square. The subtle stitching creates a dimension to the sashiko and secures the quilt sections together.

9) The quilt framework looks attractive stitched in a meandered fashion. Place the Freehand Embroidery foot on the machine and stitch the open space of border in an uniform design, working from center outward. To meander stitch, visualize the jigsaw puzzle shape. Keep the curves uniform in size by moving the fabric evenly and slowly, while pressing the foot control to sew fast. Two machine options to make machine quilting easier are *needle-down* (needle stops in the fabric) and *1/2 speed* (allows more hand control).

10) Bind the quilt with an attractive mitered corner binding (see Chapter 9).

BOOKCOVERS

Sashiko design is very complementary to the custom bookcover. Sashiko patterns can take on the flavor of complexity with multiple designs sewn on one cover, or the calmness of uniformity when one design is repeated across the yardage. Try numerous sashiko designs on denim, printed fabric or a combination of yardages, sewn together in *crazy patchwork* fashion.

SUPPLIES:

Book of choice

Yardage measured the width of book, opened on spine plus six inches (for the facings) by height of book plus one inch. *Hint:* For accurate cutting, trace around book, then add the facing/stitching measurement.

Tricot fusible interfacing to fit cover yardage

Lining - cotton print to equal sashiko yardage

Cordonnet thread in color contrast to book yardage - top

Polyester thread to match fabric - bobbin

General sewing supplies

Chalk marker and ruler

Sashiko pattern

Special accessory: Open Embroidery foot

DIRECTIONS:

1. Fuse tricot interfacing to underside of cover fabric. Mark and stitch sashiko pattern on fabric.

2. Place sashiko fabric right side up, center lining to book cover, right side down (right sides together).
   Optional: Insert grosgrain ribbon bookmark at midpoint of cover, between cover and lining.

3. Stitch 3/8 inch seam allowance across top and bottom and one side of cover, attaching lining to outside fabric. Turn, clip and press. Fold in 3/8 inch hem on remaining open side, press and edge stitch.

4. Turn book cover, outside cover facing up. Fold ends toward center, 3 1/2 inch on each end, right sides together. Stitch across each end, top and bottom, making pocket.

5. Turn right side out and insert book.

CHAPTER 9

Finishing Touches

Many times the final touch makes the difference in a project. A beautiful edge, yardage of ultimate choice, embellished surfaces and careful workmanship always define the quality difference among handcrafts. Indeed, to *stitch with a difference* defines the stitcher extraordinaire.

Each of the projects in this book could have been finished many different ways. This chapter is a connection between the sashiko patterns and individual projects found in Chapter 8, and the finishes chosen. Review the finishes, then select the ones appropriate to each design. They will set each project apart.

GATHERED PIPING

Cut crosswise yardage two to three times the length needed and wide enough to fit around cord plus 5/8 inch seam on each side. Wrap cord with fabric. Using the leather roller foot, left needle position, stitch a few inches, lower the needle into the fabric and gently pull cord while gathering casing behind the foot. Stitch gathered cord to pillow front in snug 5/8 inch seam. Finish ends, then place pillow back to front, right sides together. Sew units together, using cord stitching as a guide. Leave lower edge open to insert pillow form.

TURKISH CORNERS (GATHERED)

At each right angled corner draw a curve on the inside of the square. Repeat the curved shape on each corner of front and back pillow shapes. Stitch a row of machine basting around each curved corner, three inches each direction from center of curve. Pull basting thread up to desired gathered fullness. Arrange gathering equally to each corner, then tie tails of gathering threads. Place right sides together and stitch pillow unit, leaving lower edge open to insert pillow form.

FLOSS TIES

To fabric surface place a strand of embroidery floss. With Open Embroidery foot, satin stitch across the center of each floss strand. Begin and end with a securing stitch of 0 width and length. Looks somewhat like a tied quilt - contrast embroidery floss adds a dimension to the background fabric.

FOLDED FILET EDGING

Many times a sashiko designed pillow is complemented by a contrast color of edging placed between the sashiko designed fabric and the outer fabric border.

To make the filet insert, first cut four lengthwise strips of fabric 1/2 inch wide by each side dimension of the sashiko insert. Fold each strip in half and press. Match cut fabric edges of filet strip to sashiko cut edge. Attach filet to sashiko fabric with a 1/4 inch seam. Join the outer fabric border to the accented sashiko.

FOLDED MITERED QUILT CORNER

Cut a continuous binding strip twice the finished width one inch plus 1/2 inch by the outside linear measurement of the quilt. Fold in half and stitch to outer edge of quilt with a 1/4 inch seam. Begin stitching binding to side of quilt, then stop 1/4 inch from corner.

Fold the adjacent side binding perpendicular to the stitched side, then begin stitching at outer edge, 1/4 inch from corner (see illustration). Continue stitching down the adjacent side of quilt. Repeat on all four sides.

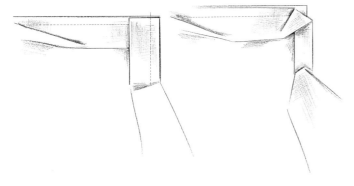

When binding is completely stitched around quilt, turn the folded edge to back of quilt. Stitch in ditch.

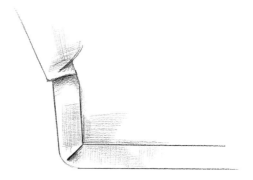

EDGE STITCHING

Edges look crisp and detailed with a thread line stitched neatly along the edge. Place the Edge Stitch foot #10 on machine and change needle position to align to near

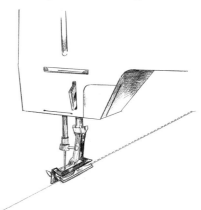

edge of fabric. Using foot center blade as a guide, stitch an even thread line around project, beginning and ending at an inconspicuous spot (example: on a garment begin at underarm seam line).

PILLOW FORM

Cut two pieces of medium weight cotton of neutral color the finished pillow size, plus one inch for each side (example: 12 inch pillow requires 14 inch cut insert). Sew together in 1/4 inch seam, leaving an opening on one edge. Turn seam inside and stuff form with polyester. Stuff firmly, then stitch opening closed.

To make the small folded triangle, find the center point of a two inch length of two inch wide ribbon. Fold from that point one side at a right angle. Fold the other side the same way. Tuck the small triangle in the lower corner of the label.

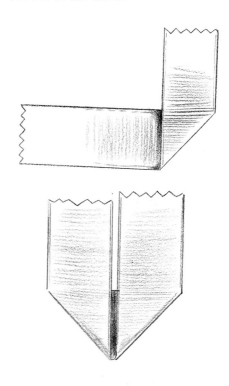

PERSONALIZED LABELS

Finish sashiko with a perfect accent - a personalized label. Utilize the special features on the machine such as the alphabet and decorative stitches. Cut and interface a four inch square of medium weight fabric and design a personal identity for sashiko clothing. Include on the label the 1) name of garment, 2) your name and 3) decorative details.

CHAPTER 10

Conclusion

Since page one the focus of adapting an ageless stitch - the running stitch - into modern technology has been explored. What delight it has been to discover the beauty of sashiko, simply the method of stitching is different, when we adapt traditional pattern to cordonnet thread and the sewing machine.

Sashiko is the simplest of stitches (the straight stitch), with each pattern limited only by the stitcher's imagination. Adaptions of fabric, thread and machine stitch to individual choices result in unique sashiko beauty. Each pattern is as new as it is old.

Thread your machine and explore. Stitch beautiful patterns in traditional white thread on indigo fabric. Enjoy the patterns as they become stronger, row after row. Add patterns that twist and curve, then try patterns strong and taut. Stretch these patterns to new horizons. Place two stitch rows together - one row red, the other purple. Change to metallic or pearl rayon thread. Sew another row in a decorative stitch of a zigzag followed by a straight, or a series of stars with the curve. Exploration of each pattern is endless; every stitch a magical discovery.

Sashiko by machine is a stitcher's journey almost completely unexplored. Enjoy every stitch as a new direction in your enduring stitcher's path.

Glossary

Batting

Loft fiber, natural or synthetic, available in different thicknesses. Used under outer fabric for warmth and density.

Black Latch Bobbin Case

An alternate bobbin case designed for use with decorative threads.

Circular Embroidery Attachment

A device placed over the feed dogs that guides stitch structures into circles.

Cordonnet Thread

Thick, cord-like twisted strand used for sewing sashiko. It is also referred to as topstitch or bottonhole twist.

Decorative Threads

As used for sashiko, refers to rayon, metallic, pearl rayon, etc. Available in different weights, fibers and colors.

Even-running Stitch

Stitches sewn with consistent length and space.

Grid Patterns

Formed with lines connecting, one to another, in geometric fashion (walkways, mosaics).

Indigo

A deep pigment blue dye used to color plain weave fabric; sometimes indigo is referenced as the fabric.

Interfacing

A fabric placed under yardage to provide body and substance to garment.

Interfacing, Fusible

A lightweight yardage (with sashiko, often knit tricot) with a fabric adhesive on one side. Heat applied to knit fusible and outer fabric joins the units as one.

Marking Tools

Chalks, fabric pencils, masking tape, etc. used to transfer designs to fabric.

Measuring Tools

Rulers, curves, circle templates, etc. used to mark accurate designs to fabric.

Motif Patterns

Distinctive shapes adapted from floral, animal, crest, etc.

Patchwork

Designs formed from different shapes put together. In this resource, reference is made to traditional American quilt patterns - *Jacob's Ladder, Nine-patch,* etc.

Plain-weave Fabric

Equal number of threads are woven over/under one another.

Pouncer

Cloth square filled with powder, then tied. Used to transfer design through a perforated pattern.

Pre-shrink

Washing yardage prior to cutting and stitching to prevent undesirable shrinkage after project is finished.

Sashiko

A Japanese stitch form utilizing the running stitch. Grid and motif patterns were traditionally sewn with a soft, thick cotton thread on indigo yardage.

Stencil

A thin sheet of paper or plastic printed with a design, then pierced to permit chalk or powder to be rubbed through openings, transferring design to another surface.

Straighten Yardage

Redirect (by pulling) the warp (lengthwise) and weft (crosswise) threads of yardage to perfect right angles.

Topstitch Needle

Designed with an oversized eye; suitable for a thicker thread.

Twill-weave Fabric

Woven to create a visible diagonal line across yardage.

Underlining

Cut exactly like the outer fabric, it adds crispness and contour to project. Helps prevent wrinkling and stretching.

References

Benjamin, Bonnie. *The Quilting of Japan - From Tradition to Today*. Glendale, CA, 1987.

D'Addetta, Joseph. *Traditional Japanese Design Motifs*. Dover Publications, Inc., 1984.

Hornung, Clarence. *Traditional Japanese Stencil Designs*. New York: Dover Publications, Inc., 1985.

Kasuri Dyeworks. (*Assorted Japanese titles*). Berkeley, CA.

Liddell, Jill and Yuko Watanabe. *Japanese Quilts*. New York: E.P. Dutton.

Matseunaga, Karen Kim. *Japanese Country Quilting*. Toyoko: Kodansha Int. Ltd., 1990.

Mende, Kazuko and Reiko Morishige. *Sashiko: Blue & White Quilt Art of Japan*. New York: Kodansha America, Inc., 1991.

Ogawa, Hiroko. "*Embroidery From Japanese Snow Country*," Threads, XVIII, Aug/Sept, 1988, 22>.

Ota, Kimi. *Sashiko Quilting*. Seattle, Washington, 1981.

Rostocki, Janet. *Sashiko - Japanese Style Quilting*. Dayton, Ohio: Summa Design, 1988.

Sashiko - Traditional Japanese Quilt Designs. Toyoko: Niko Vogue Publishing, Ltd., 1989.

The Classic Quilting of Sashiko. Toyoko: Ondorisha Publishers, Ltd., 1990.

Useful Addresses

BERNINA OF AMERICA, INC.
534 W. Chestnut
Hinsdale, IL 60521
*sewing machines, sergers,
Create-a-Space tables*

BUTTERICK COMPANY, INC.
161 Avenue of the Americas
New York, NY 10013
patterns

CLOVER NEEDLECRAFT INC.
1007 E. Domnquez St., Suite L
Carson, CA 40746
marking tools, chalk

DAN RIVER, INC.
111 West 40th Street
New York, NY 10018
denim

FAIRFIELD PROCESSING CORP.
88 Rose Hill Avenue
P.O. Box 1157
Danbury, CT 06810
stuffing and batting

FOLKWEAR PATTERNS
The Taunton Press, Inc.
63 S. Main Street
P.O. Box 5506
Newton, CT 06740
ethnic patterns

HANDLER TEXTILE CORP.
450 Seventh Avenue
New York, NY 10123
woven/non-woven interfacings

KASURI DYEWORKS
1959 Shattuck Avenue
Berkeley, CA 94704
*assorted Japanese titles, fabrics
and supplies*

MADEIRA MARKETING LTD.
600 East 9th
Michigan City, IN 46360
decorative threads

NEEDLEARTS INTERNATIONAL
P.O. Box 6447
Glendale, CA 91225
books, stencils

OMNIGRID, INC.
3227-B 164th SW
Lynnwood, WA 98037
rulers

SPRINGMAID FABRICS
Div. Springs Industries
104 West 40th Street
New York, NY 10018
muslin, fashion prints

SULKY OF AMERICA
3113 Broadpoint Drive
Harbor Heights, FL 33983
rayon threads

WM. E. WRIGHT
South Street
West Warren, MA 01092
*cordonnet, polyester, silk-finish
cotton threads*

YLI CORPORATION
45 West 300 North
Provo, UT 84601
pearl rayon threads

Autobiography of the Author

Since 1986 I have blended my background in teaching clothing and textiles into a teaching, writing and designing format with the educational team at Bernina of America, Inc.

Only last year did I question the validity of my decision to leave the traditional classroom and the universal plan of the 24 hour day. After Bernina and I reached the agreement on my authorship of the sashiko book did I discover chapter deadlines still come due in spite of:

- The monthly travel and teaching responsibilities at quilt conferences from Washington to Texas.

- The hectic spring move with my family down the state of Texas to a village of 1500.

- The transition of helping Charles to open a specialty retail shop for his multi-artistic talents.

- Monthly magazine projects and copy commitments with clockwork deadlines that happened only with my cooperative and understanding (thank goodness) editors in the sewing industry.

And best of all, I discovered near the book completion, there is a saneness in the 24 hour day. Our family began to find roots, our retail shop opened on schedule, and our friends have found us in our tiny village. They come to Salado to see the shops, the creek, and best of all, me and mine, as we live from one deadline to another.

MOTIF PATTERNS

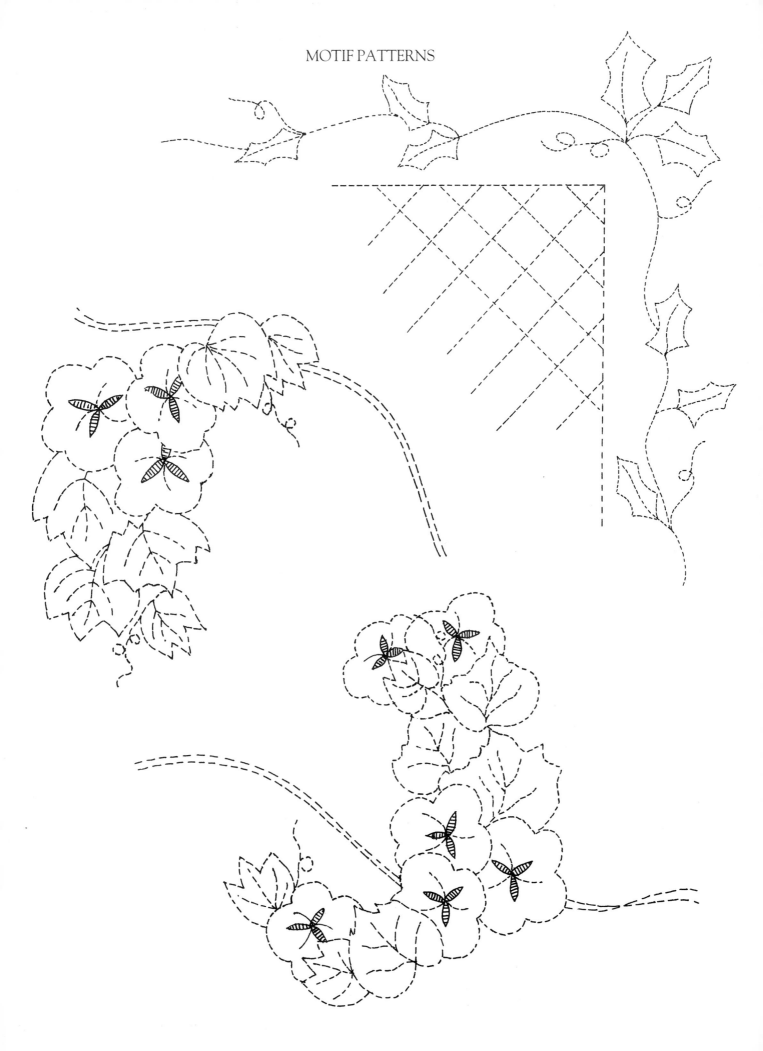